'Lucid prose ... an Orwellian dislike of cant, moral relativism and sloppy thinking ... black humour.'
The Oldie

'Dalrymple is... [o]ne of the most interesting men of our times... There is nothing in his tale to celebrate, yet in the telling he deserves the commendation of anybody who values human civilisation.'
The Times

'Nobody has observed the... fallacies of modern England with a clearer eye, or a more intelligent quill. It would be nice to know that the BBC had heard of him because we could expect to hear him deliver next year's Reith Lectures.'
Sunday Telegraph

'A razor-sharp expose of our broken society... One of the greatest men of our age... Both funny and a badly needed corrective to conventional wisdom... hugely readable ... gripping real-life stories... tells a deep truth about the sort of society we have become. A future historian, a century hence, will learn more about 21st-century Britain from this book than from any official document. So will you. Please read it.'
Peter Hitchens, *Mail on Sunday*

'For anyone interested in the real world of ciminals and the criminal mind, there is no more essential writer than Theodore Dalrymple... Performs a national service by revealing - with cold, precise rage - the follies of the bureaucracy that envelops our penal system. The blackest of blac'

The Knife Went In

A Prison Doctor on Britain's Dark Side

THEODORE DALRYMPLE

London

GIBSON SQUARE

This edition first published in 2018.

rights@gibsonsquare.com
www.gibsonsquare.com

ISBN   9781783341207
eISBN   9781783341191

The moral right of Theodore Dalrymple to be identified as the author of this work has been asserted in accordance with the Copyright, Designs and Patents Act 1988.

Papers used by Gibson Square are natural, recyclable products made from wood grown in sustainable forests; inks used are vegetable based. Manufacturing conforms to ISO 14001, and is accredited to FSC and PEFC chain of custody schemes. Colour-printing is through a certified CarbonNeutral® company that offsets its CO2 emissions.

Printed by Clays Ltd.

Contents

Preamble: Oh to Be in Britain   7

1	The Knife Went In	21
2	Desperate, Wild and Furious	27
3	Decision Time	42
4	Sticks and Stones	56
5	Prison Officers	70
6	The Money of Frauds	83
7	Suicides	100
8	Dr No	115
9	Encouraging Thwacks	129
10	Rule Forty Five	137
11	The Thin Blue Squiggle	167
12	Recent Activity in Homicides	180
13	Psychiatric Fungus	195
14	No Good Act...	208
15	Loud Pleasures	214
16	A Simple Caution	227
17	Drunken Stress	241
18	Malevolent Characters	254
19	Manic Mitigations	268

Pride Goeth...   279

Preamble
Oh to Be in Britain

Two cases together can illuminate a whole society, as flashes of lightning light up a landscape on a dark night. Not that the first, the case of Ched Evans in 2016 tells us something entirely new about British society. Ched, or Chedwyn, Evans was a Welsh professional soccer player, not yet of the highest rank but still, at 23, earning over one million pounds a year. He decided to have a weekend in his hometown of Rhyl, a seaside resort on the north coast of Wales in 2011. He was accompanied by a friend from earlier in his career, a soccer player of the same age named Clayton McDonald, as well as by another few friends and his half-brother. They went to a club called the Zu Bar — an appropriate enough name in view of what some of them were about to do — but split up after leaving at about 2:30 am. Evans had booked a local hotel room for McDonald, who later sent a text informing him that he had taken a girl there.

Evans decided to join him in the hotel. He managed to persuade the receptionist to let him have a key to McDonald's room, which he then entered without knocking. McDonald was having sex with the young woman and, according to Evans, asked her whether his friend could join in. McDonald claims that it was Evans who asked. They both maintained that she consented. A charming feature of the story is that Evans's half-brother and one of his friends went with him to the hotel, where they attempted to film the sexual proceedings on their cell phones from outside the bedroom window. But they didn't get far: Evans was delicate enough to close the curtains before he undressed. When McDonald had finished with the young woman, Evans took over, as in a relay, and McDonald left the hotel room.

Then Evans, who, according to his own later account, said not another word to her before, during, or after his intercourse with her — though she asked him to go harder at it — suddenly remembered that he was betraying his girlfriend of eighteen months, desisted from sex, dressed, and left by the hotel fire escape. Practically everything in Britain that happens outdoors is now captured on closed-circuit television, in a dubious attempt to promote public order, and he was seen on film, slinking away like a thief in the night.

The young woman, nineteen, woke naked in bed the next morning, unaware of where she was and not remembering how she had gotten there. Her amnesia for the second half of the previous evening was total, but as she had drunk two large glasses of wine (amounting to two-thirds of a bottle), four double shots of vodka, and a Sambuca, she thought her drinks must have been spiked to have produced this degree of amnesia. She had drunk more than this on other occasions, she said, without blacking out. She was distressed in general by waking up in a strange place with no knowledge of how she had gotten there, and now she discovered that her bag was missing. It was of this that she went to the police to complain.

She made no allegations of rape against the two men (how could she, if she remembered nothing?), but the police soon traced both Evans and McDonald. Interviewed by the police, Evans volunteered an account of the sexual escapade and told the police that they could have had any of the girls in the bar that evening because they were soccer players and rich, and that that was what the girls liked. As a sociological generalisation, this observation might have been at least partly true; but in the circumstances, it was an unwise, as well as a crude, thing to say. The police charged the two men with rape, on the grounds that the young woman was in no condition to give consent to sexual intercourse, and that they either knew, or ought to have known, that this was the case.

The impetus for the charges came entirely from the prosecuting authorities; the alleged victim at no point claimed to have been raped. Toxicological evidence was unilluminating: by the time blood was taken from the young woman, her blood-alcohol level had declined to zero; no substance with which her drinks might have been spiked was present. She exhibited traces of both cannabis and cocaine, compatible with her having taken them several days before the night in question. The first trial produced a verdict that at first might seem puzzling: McDonald was acquitted and Evans found guilty.

There was no plausible pharmacological explanation of how the woman might have been able to give consent to McDonald but not to Evans. But to secure a verdict of guilty in such cases, it must be shown not only that the woman was incapable of giving consent but that the accused had no reasonable grounds for belief that she could give consent. In McDonald's case, the alleged victim had gone back to the hotel with him in a taxi, which she had voluntarily entered; this gave him some reason for believing that she had consented to having sex, which Evans, who entered the room unasked and unannounced, lacked. This was so even if McDonald was mistaken in his belief; and this might have been the decisive difference between the two men in the jury's mind.

Evans received a sentence of five years' imprisonment, which means, in our deceiving times in which nothing means what it appears to mean, that he would be let out after two and a half years, as, in fact, he was. From the first, he maintained his innocence, and, because he refused to acknowledge his guilt and jump through the prescribed hoops that sex offenders must jump through, he endured a harder prison regime than he would otherwise have been subjected to.

Now consider the other case with quite a different cast of characters — this one in Derby. An unemployed man, Michael Philpott (in his fifties), fathered seventeen children by four women, all of whom he treated violently. For ten years, he lived in one house with two of these women: his wife, Mairead, with whom he had six children and had recently taken up dogging — which had got her pregnant by one of the anonymous participants; and his concubine, Lisa Willis, with whom he had four children. Tired of Philpott's abuse, Willis left him in 2012 and took her children with her. Philpott, furious at this insubordination, wanted the children back. He, his wife, and a friend hatched a plot: they would set fire to the house in which his six children by his wife were asleep; Philpott would rush in and save them, showing himself to be a heroic and devoted father. He would then blame the departed Willis for setting the fire, which would result in her going to prison and his winning custody of her children. But the plan went catastrophically wrong: the fire got out of hand, and all six children died, five by asphyxiation and one by burns.

The bizarre, malevolent plot was quickly exposed. It also came to light that all involved had long lived on government subsidies. In the trial that followed, the prosecution alleged that Philpott had wanted custody of Willis's five children — the four whom he had fathered and one by another man — because of the welfare benefits attached to them. When Philpott lived with the two women, the household was receiving about £60,000 a year in such benefits, as well as money that both women earned in part-time jobs. Willis' departure, then, meant almost halving the household's welfare income — which, evidence suggested, Philpott used as much for his own pleasures as for the benefit of his progeny.

The revelations set off a furious debate about the indiscriminate nature of state welfare with a headline about Philpott that has since become notorious: 'VILE PRODUCT OF WELFARE BRITAIN'. The then Chancellor of the Exchequer George Osborne remarked, rather mildly in the circumstances, that the case raised questions about the propriety of subsidising the lifestyles of Philpott and of people who lived as he did.

Indignant responses followed from defenders of the welfare system. The Labour Party accused the chancellor of using a tragic case for low political ends. A well-known journalist, Owen Jones, observed that only 190 cases were known in which people dependent on benefits had ten or more children, adding that Philpott's example told us no more about welfare recipients than the case of Harold Shipman, a doctor who murdered as many as 200 of his elderly patients, told us about the medical profession. Unusually, Jones — who believes in the social causation of almost everything — blamed the children's deaths entirely on Philpott, calling him a 'monster.' A curious ideological reversal had taken place: those who normally made individuals accountable for their conduct blamed society (in the form of the welfare state) for the crime; those who normally blamed society blamed the individual. On the whole, the debate generated more heat than light, becoming, as so many things do, a media frenzy.

The welfare system as currently constituted was almost certainly a necessary condition for much of Philpott's conduct, though, of course, not a sufficient one. Philpott was able-bodied and capable of work. Even before the arson case made him infamous, he had appeared twice on television programs — first requesting larger public housing for his family, and then being told that the TV show had found three jobs for him. He showed up for none. By then, the generous benefit system had rendered work economically an own goal; his children had become his milk cows. But while the state had made his conduct possible — and profitable — it did not require it. The great majority of people on welfare do not behave as he did, as Jones rightly noted.

Second, just as hard cases make bad law, so the extreme consequences of a system can lead one to draw hasty lessons. Any system involving large numbers of people will include extreme cases of almost anything that one can think of. To assess the significance of an individual story, then, we must study the meanings, beliefs, and purposes of the particular people involved in it. A biographical approach is essential.

And Philpott's biography does indeed shed light on his actions. One notices, to begin with, that the extreme frivolity of the English criminal-justice system facilitated his conduct at least as much as the welfare system did. And no doubt the defects of the two systems are related. For example, they share a view that people, especially at the lower end of the social scale, are the helpless creatures of bad circumstances unlike a soccer player on one million pounds a year such as Ched Evans. This is a view that quickly communicates itself to the people of whom it is believed, and who then come to believe it themselves or use it to extract the maximum benefit from the systems in question.

As a young man, Philpott almost killed his girlfriend when she told him that she was leaving him. Already displaying the jealousy and possessiveness that would mark his later behaviour, the twenty-one-year-old stabbed her multiple times, rupturing her bladder and her liver and puncturing her lung. She was fortunate to survive. When her mother tried to intervene, Philpott stabbed and injured her as well. The attack was not just an isolated adolescent outburst but a sign of a thoroughly bad character. In past incidents, the young Philpott had fractured his girlfriend's patella with a hammer and shot her in the groin with a crossbow. After the stabbing, authorities charged him with attempted murder and grievous bodily harm, for both of which the maximum legal penalty in England is life imprisonment. Instead of the maximum, Philpott received a sentence of seven years' imprisonment and was released after serving only three years and two months — in other words just over half a year longer than Ched Evans for his rape conviction for non-consensual intercourse.

But that was not the end of the indulgence of the criminal-justice system in Philpott's case. When he attracted the law's attention for acts of violence several more times, no inference was made that he remained a dangerous man. In 2010, for example, the police 'cautioned' him for striking his wife and dragging her out of the house by her hair. It is true that a petty criminal who repeats his petty crimes may not become dangerous; but a man who has committed a dangerous crime and continues to commit lesser crimes is likely to return to dangerous crime, especially in England, where the police have a poor success rate at detecting perpetrators.

If the criminal-justice system had worked properly, Philpott would never have been at liberty to father, let alone kill, his children. A very long imprisonment for his first brutal crimes would not have been unfair or disproportionate given their gravity; and even if he had been released from prison earlier, it should have been on the understanding that if he ever so much as laid a finger on anyone again, he would spend at least the rest of the sentence behind bars.

Instead, Philpott learned that nearly killing someone was of little account in the eyes of the law — an impression strengthened by the passage of time, as the memory of his three years in prison became foreshortened and as repeated acts of violence on his part met with slaps on the wrist.

Another significant feature of Philpott's life worth noting in this context is the ease — not unlike that of a young, well-remunerated soccer player — with which he attracted young women. And then violently abused them. Though the number of children he fathered was far from typical, Philpott's abusive behaviour was not statistically unusual. Jealousy and possessiveness have always belonged to the human repertoire of feeling and action, especially among men. Over the years, the number of Philpott-types went gradually up in the inner-city hospital and prison where I worked, at least in respect to their conduct toward women. Even more interesting is that I also saw more and more Philpott-type women, whose jealousy and possessiveness toward men manifested itself in precisely the same violent way.

Philpott, too, lived in a part of society in which sexual mores had loosened, without the desire for exclusive sexual possession having diminished — rather the reverse. Philpott is not a typical product of these developments but their apotheosis: and apotheoses have their heuristic value. Not the welfare system alone, not judicial leniency alone, and not the jealousy consequent upon the sexual revolution alone produced Philpott; but all went into the witches' brew from which he emerged. And he emerged from it not as something resembling an automatic and inevitable chemical reaction but rather as a human being reacting consciously to his environment and circumstances. When Owen Jones called Philpott a monster, he was perfectly correct, and monsters there will always be, simply because of inherent human variation; but he was a monster who met a congenial system in which monsters could flourish (if you can call how he lived flourishing).

At the same time, Ched Evans's girlfriend Natasha Massey stuck by him. The daughter of a rich businessman, she funded a sophisticated campaign on Evans' behalf. It included a website that showed a video of the young woman entering the hotel not in such a state of intoxication that she would have been obviously incapable of giving consent: and drunken consent is still consent. Another video, taken before she arrived at the hotel, purportedly showed her urinating in the street. A cousin of Evans not only named her on social media (which was illegal) but also called her 'a drunken slut.'

Judges twice refused Evans's request for an appeal of conviction; they saw no new grounds for overturning the verdict. On his third attempt, he was granted a retrial because new evidence had come to light. Two men came forward to testify that the young woman had earlier behaved with them in a very specific sexual way, precisely as Evans had claimed during the first trial. A woman's previous sexual activity is not admissible in rape trials: promiscuity does not imply a general consent to all and sundry.

The appeals court ruled in this case, however, that the evidence was so specific that it was admissible and, if offered to the jury, might result in a different verdict — as, in the event, it did. The fact that one of the new witnesses described the alleged victim behaving sexually exactly as Evans had described — she had demanded certain practices of the three men — as well as being amnesic the following morning, was particularly useful to the defence. It contradicted her own testimony that she had never had amnesia before.

Evans did not substantially alter his original evidence at his retrial. The prosecution tried to cast doubt on the testimony of the two men because Massey had offered a reward of £50,000 for any evidence leading to Evans's acquittal. But the jury, composed of seven women and five men, either believed the evidence or at least placed enough credence on it to conclude that the prosecution had failed to prove its case beyond a reasonable doubt. Both the judge and the defence counsel at the retrial were women, incidentally; the prosecutor was male. Evans was acquitted by unanimous verdict after only two hours' deliberation. He is thus no longer a rapist and will not have to spend the rest of his life on a registry of sex offenders. When Evans was released from prison, still a convicted rapist, his former soccer club, Sheffield United, proposed to reemploy him. This caused considerable outrage, and an online petition soon garnered 160,000 signatures. Prominent supporters of the club threatened to withdraw their support. The tone of commentary was mostly vengeful.

Just as a secret is what you tell only one other person, so every penological liberal has just one crime that he wants severely punished, cannot forgive, and for which there can be no adequate penance. Evans had committed it, or so it then seemed; he was therefore to be prevented from pursuing his career.

That this vengefulness was the main motive of the objection to Evans's playing soccer again is suggested by the fact that Clayton McDonald's career was more comprehensively and finally ruined than was Evans's. Unlike Evans, McDonald had been acquitted at the first trial — yet he had, in effect, been convicted by the public of a crime from which there could be no exoneration. As a well-known political figure once said, if you sling enough mud, some of it sticks.

Yet those who maintained Evans' innocence were no less vengeful. Despite the fact that the allegations against him came entirely from police and prosecuting authorities — which Evans himself has always recognized — the young woman at the centre of the case faced a barrage of abuse and insult on social media. No evidence ever came to light that she was seeking to make money from the sordid affair, as commonly stated by her critics, some of whom revealed her whereabouts, so that she felt it necessary to move and change her identity five times. Evans never took part in or sanctioned any of this inexcusable activity.

As alarming as was the viciousness of many people, even worse was the revelation of how little people either understood or cared about the rule of law. The *Guardian*, normally of the forgive-them-for-they-know-not-what-they-do school of justice, published several articles in the wake of Evans's final acquittal that indicated that the authors would prefer someone to be wrongly imprisoned and to carry a legal stigma for life, even though found to be not guilty. One of these articles alleged that Evans was acquitted only because he was well funded. It is however a fair presumption that the jury did not acquit him on the grounds that he was rich but on the grounds that the prosecution failed to put its case beyond reasonable doubt. The lesson in the Evans case, if any, might then be that in cases of rape in which the evidence boils down to one person's word against another's, all other evidence for the prosecution and defence having cancelled each other out, convictions are likely to be unsafe, but only the rich have the means to prove them so.

Irrespective of their final legal outcomes, both supremely sordid stories are emblematic of a prevalent aspect of contemporary British culture. No one who has gone down the main street of a British town at midnight on Friday could really have been much surprised by either incident. Evans has acknowledged that his behaviour was bad, though (perhaps understandably) without recognition of just how disgusting it was. But it would be implausible to say that the conduct of the alleged victim at the time was well beyond reproach. What about the crown prosecution or public opinion, did they at least walk with angels…?

As for Michael Philpott, or how the authorities dealt with his egregious and persistent criminal behaviour, what more is there to add…?

The Knife Went In

I have met quite a number of murderers as a prison GP and psychiatrist. Often they don't quite appear to be who they are. The most notorious murderer whom I have ever met was Frederick West. In a small house in Gloucester, he and his wife, Rosemary, had sexually tortured, murdered, dismembered, and buried twelve people, including two of their own children. Their crimes came to light in 1994, more than twenty years after they had committed the first of them; their depravity shocked even a generation sated with criminal sensation. When I first encountered West, he seemed affable, spending much of his time playing pool with the prison officers — though there was something sinister and lycanthropic about him, even when he tried to be deferential and charming.

I was a very young doctor when I met my first murderer, a man in late middle age who strangled his wife because (he said) she would not leave him to read his evening paper in peace when he returned home from work, and in talking her little drop-earrings jiggled most provokingly. Without criminal antecedents, it was thought he must be mad and was sent to hospital rather than prison. I felt honoured to shake so bad a man's hand, never having met anyone half as wicked before.

He, it turned out, was almost the only murderer I was ever to meet who resembled slightly the reputable type described by Orwell in his essay, 'The Decline of the English Murder', whom the English so liked to read about between the wars. This type of murderer was respectable, even religious, middle- or lower-middle class, leading something of a double life, and impelled either by greed for the life insurance he had taken out on his victim or the need to cover up an illicit affair. The only two murderers whom I met who killed for life insurance waited no longer than two weeks after the sum assured was increased dramatically before disposing of their victims, thus providing something of a clue as to their motivation.

I did however observe a peculiarly modern phenomenon in the prison where I first started working as a doctor — the prisoner's use of the passive voice as a means of distancing himself from his own decisions, and of persuading others of his lack of responsibility for his actions. I noticed the phenomenon when speaking to murderers who had stabbed someone to death and who invariably said, 'the knife went in,' as if it were the knife that guided the hand rather than the hand that guided the knife.

Such a murderer may have crossed the city, taking a knife with him, to confront the very person against whom he bore a serious grudge. Yet still it was the knife that went in. When I relayed this observation to my wife, also a doctor, she thought I was exaggerating. But one day she was in her clinic when she asked an elderly widow how her husband had met his death. 'The knife went in,' the widow said. My wife, astounded, waited for the end of the consultation to telephone me to tell me what she had heard her say.

I subsequently noticed that all prisoners used similar locutions, though only to describe their bad behaviour, never their good behaviour. 'The beer went mad' or 'the beer took over' were phrases that alcoholics favoured, as if the beer drank them rather than the other way round. Heroin addicts, describing how and why they started to take heroin, almost invariably said that they 'fell in with the wrong crowd.' When I replied that I found it strange that I met many people who fell in with the wrong crowd, but never any member of the wrong crowd itself, they invariably laughed. Foolishness is not the same as stupidity.

Of course, like the modern criminal we are all guilty of the method from time to time. We seek freedom from the moral responsibility of our worst acts, which is why *The Knife Went In* is the title of this book — or at least one reason.

Prison language has continued to fascinate me. It is always vivid and expressive, and, in a way, beautiful. 'My head's cabbaged' meant that a person was in such a tormented state that he was not fully responsible for his actions. 'You're not going to nut me off, are you, doctor?' was a fearful enquiry as to whether I was going to send the prisoner to a psychiatric hospital (psychiatric wards in the NHS are infinitely worse than prison). A prisoner who had just been sentenced to life imprisonment would say, 'the judge lifed me off.'

In contrast, the crimes of the great majority of the

murderers whom I encountered were merely sordid. A drunken or drug-intoxicated quarrel over nothing, such were the circumstances of most those crimes. The most trivial pretext of a murder I encountered was a remark about the brand of trainers the perpetrator was wearing, which he considered humiliating. This no doubt is powerful testimony to the tender egos, of some of our fellow citizens, inflamed by their subordinate position in the world. The people in prison are very far removed from the social atmosphere in which a man may kill a woman and then play 'Nearer my God to thee' on a harmonium next door.

I still hoped that one day I would be called in as an expert on an Agatha Christie-type murder, a vicar who had poisoned a squire in a library, for example, but I never was. Most likely this was because not many vicars poison squires in libraries these days.

George Orwell was in fact hardly the first person to notice the decline in the English murder — in its quality, that is, not the quantity. Virginia Woolf's father, Sir Leslie Stephen, did so as long ago as 1869, at the very commencement of what Orwell thought was the golden age of English murder, when petty bourgeois non-conformist religious hypocrisy set the tenor of the times.

The more typical circumstances for a modern murder are for example one involving a squalid quarrel over a £10 debt. Or rather, it was committed in an attempt to recover that debt. There are still corners of our society — not as small, perhaps, as we should like to imagine — in which such sums are deemed worth fighting over, and even killing for.

In the city where the murdered man lived, he was one of

the unemployed who formed a common sort of informal drinking club in which the members staggered the days of their receipt of social security so that they could buy drink throughout the week. He had borrowed £10 during a drinking bout that he declined to repay. The other four members of the club, one of them a woman of about thirty, went to extract the money from him. It was she I was asked to examine, in a case of psychiatric extenuation. It was suggested by her lawyer that she might be mentally deficient.

Her defence was that she had done nothing, that she was only a bystander. It was they who had killed him. They all claimed the same thing, of course. But what violence. The four of them turned the victim's flat in a tower block into a torture chamber. The victim, besides being an alcoholic, was disabled, close to heart failure, and able to move to and from his electrically-reclining chair only with difficulty. That made it easier to torture him. They broke his legs, they broke his ribs (all of them), they fractured his skull. They boiled kettles and poured the water over him. Still no £10.

Eventually, they concluded that he really didn't have the money. He wasn't just trying to 'blag' them, as the local expression has it, and the four left the flat together to go for a drink, having already consumed what was in his flat. They left him alive, but only just. He must have died within the hour.

Astonishingly, as with Fred West I could not completely dislike the accused. Being sober in prison had done wonders for her.

She felt no guilt, because she had been only a bystander, but nor did she appear much disturbed by what she had witnessed. She said she did not leave and call for help because the others wouldn't let her. But what about the drinks afterwards?

'I was afraid not to go with them.'

The defence suggested that she might not be intelligent enough to follow a trial, and although I thought that she was, I suggested a formal intelligence test. There were two psychologists who worked in the prison in which she was held, but they refused to carry out the test. Indeed, they seemed rather put out that I had asked, as if they were heart surgeons asked to cut toenails. They were not paid to do it, they said, but gave me the number of a private psychologist. The trouble was that she wanted to charge so much that neither the prosecution nor defence would stand the cost.

I thus tested the cognitive ability of the accused myself. Among other things, I asked her whether she remembered anything recently in the news. As it happens, a particularly vicious and psychopathic woman had just been sentenced to life imprisonment for the stabbing to death of three men. It is usually men who commit such crimes. 'Yes,' she said, 'there was that terrible woman in the papers what killed three men.'

And she added, 'I don't know what this world's coming to.'

1

Desperate, Wild and Furious

There is a permanent tension between regarding men as individuals and as members of a class of men. From the fact that boys from Stratford did not generally go off to be actors in London, one might conclude that Shakespeare was never an actor in London. And from the fact that his work is unique in world literature, one might conclude that its author could not possibly have existed.

Murder is the worst crime, of course, but similarly murderers are not necessarily the worst individuals. It is disconcerting to find oneself liking a person who has strangled someone with his bare hands, but this happened to me often in my career as a psychiatrist and prison doctor. It is not that I thought, 'There but for the grace of God go I'. I have never wanted to strangle anyone, however lost my temper. But most people are not wholly defined by the single worst act of their lives, which may however be their only act of any public significance — there is always more to them than that.

Some murderers are beyond the reach of natural sympathy,

to be sure. I remember a man who, twelve years before, had impaled three children on railings because they had made too much noise; he was baby-sitting them while he wanted to watch television. A man of limited imagination, he could not see even after many years in prison that he had done anything wrong. He threatened a medical colleague of mine with death because he refused to prescribe him sleeping tablets. He was evidently one prisoner who would never be released and, in so far as he had nothing to lose by committing another murder, his threat was not taken lightly (he was swiftly moved to another prison).

Such a man as he raises important metaphysical questions which to this day are unanswered and, being philosophical in nature, are perhaps unanswerable. He was almost certainly what would once have been designated 'morally insane'; a century later he would have been called a 'psychopath' (a phrase coined by the German psychiatrist J. Koch at the end of the 19th century), then a 'sociopath'; nowadays he would be called a sufferer from 'antisocial personality disorder' — psychiatrists think they are advancing knowledge and understanding when they change terminology.

From the very first moment he was able to act at his own volition, he would invariably have chosen to do those things that would most have distressed, disgusted or frightened others around him. He would, for example, have been cruel to animals, putting cats in washing machines and dousing dogs with petrol. He would have lied almost as a matter of principle, and stolen from those to whom he owed most duty. If intelligent he would have been able to avoid the consequences of his acts, but no punishment would in any case have corrected him or deterred him from repetition.

This pattern of development has been recognised for a long time, well before it was labelled by psychiatrists. Richard III's mother, the Duchess of York, tells him:

> Thou cams't on earth to make the earth my hell.
> A grievous burden was thy birth to me:
> Tetchy and wayward was thy infancy,
> Thy school days, frightful, desperate, wild and furious;
> Thy prime of manhood, daring, bold, and venturous;
> Thy age confirm'd, proud, subtle, sly and bloody,
> More mild, and yet more harmful, kind in hatred.

It is not that the psychopath, at least the more intelligent sort, does not know the language of morality; it is more that morality itself finds no echo in him. It means no more to him than the curious custom of a distant and obscure tribe means to the reader of an anthropological text.

Except, that is, when he finds himself the object of a perceived injustice, to which he may be exquisitely sensitive, and which he may use as a justification (to himself and others) for further crimes and misdemeanours. Richard III explains his evil by the fact that he was sent into this breathing world scarce half-made up, and so lame and unfashionable that dogs barked at him in the streets as he stopped by them; and therefore, since he could not be a lover, he was determined to prove a villain. Yet within a very short time he seduces a woman for whose husband's and father-in-law's death he was recently responsible. So much for his deformity preventing him from being a lover.

The eminent professor of developmental psychopathology, Simon Baron-Cohen, suggests that persistently evil men may have some neurological damage or deficit, and presents brain-scan evidence that this is so. But this leaves the philosophical problem largely untouched. People who are evil (or in Baron-Cohen's less emotive language, lack 'empathy') may have brain scans of type X; but does this mean that people with brain scans of type X are evil? The fact that London taxi drivers have altered brain scans after they have committed the street plan of the capital to memory does not mean that their altered brain scans are the cause of their knowledge of London or of their choice of career.

Moreover, like everyone else, Baron-Cohen is reduced to the language of morality. The subtitle of his book is *A New Theory of Human Cruelty*. Obviously, like everyone else, he believes that cruelty is morally undesirable. But no sifting of brain scans, no number of scientific examinations, will ever resolve the question of what is morally desirable or reprehensible. We cannot put a man in a scanner to find out whether or not the lie he told was justified. Baron-Cohen speaks of 'appropriate' empathy, or the lack thereof, but 'appropriateness' is not a measurable quality of the physical world. There is no instrument, no matter how sensitive, that could ever determine it. If someone empathised, say, with Mengele, would we put him in a scanner to find out whether it was right or wrong of him to do so?

It is easy to get in a terrible muddle over psychopathy. The difficulty lies in transposing general conclusions about mental disorders from scientific test results to the specifics of a real-life situation, particularly where someone has committed a crime.

I was once an expert witness retained by the prosecution in the trial for murder of a young man of limited intellect who lived in a kind of dosshouse which occupied several floors of a dilapidated building. Like the other residents, he drank a lot and misused tranquillisers, notably Valium (diazepam).

He had had a dispute with another resident whom he accused of stealing the gold chain he put round his neck. One evening this resident had retired early to bed on the top floor of the house, drunk as usual. There was a drinking party on the ground floor in which the accused took part. The drink fuelled his resentment against the other resident and he climbed the narrow and rickety stairs to administer him a beating, after which he returned to the party.

Further drink inflamed him, and he again climbed the stairs to administer a worse beating, this time with fatal results. He again returned to the party, though whether he was aware or not that the other resident was dead could not be established with any certainty.

It was accepted by the defence that the accused *had* climbed the stairs and *had* beaten the man to death — of that there was no possible doubt. The only questions remaining were whether he was actually capable of forming the intent to kill and then whether he had any abnormality of mind that substantially reduced his responsibility for his acts. (In fact, it was at that time necessary in law only to prove that he had the intention seriously to injure, for if a man dies of injuries intended only seriously to injure him, the culprit is still guilty of murder. This means that murder was a charge easier to prove than attempted murder, where it is necessary to prove that he actually intended to kill rather than merely injure.)

The prosecution had asked me to prepare a report only on whether the young man had been capable of forming the intent to kill when he in fact killed, and on no other question. The prosecuting counsel, an eminent QC, told me that my report was the shortest he had ever read, and I don't think (at least I tell myself so) that he meant this as a criticism. I wrote approximately as follows:

> The fact that the accused climbed the stairs twice and severely beat the only man on the premises against whom he had a grudge suggests that he was capable of forming an intent to kill.

Whether he actually did so was, of course, not for me to say; that was a matter for the court.

I was present at the trial only in case I was needed in rebuttal of the defence's expert evidence. In its attempt to prove that the accused was not fully responsible for his actions, the defence called an eminent professor who had made psychopaths and psychopathy the object of his life's study.

Under English law every man is sane and in control of his faculties unless proved otherwise (on a balance of probabilities). The onus of proof is on the defence that he wasn't in control at the time; the prosecution has to prove nothing, not even that the accused had a motive, though it often helps its case if it can prove a motive. A motiveless crime raises suspicions of insanity; but in murder cases motives are usually obvious.

The professor stepped into the witness box. He cut an impressive figure, tall, upright and confident. All went well with his evidence-in-chief, that is to say when he was questioned by the advocate who had called him. He was able to dilate on his opinion without contradiction, having first given his impressive qualifications, experience, research and publications.

Things fell apart during cross-examination. Calmly and without any outward sign of hostility, prosecuting counsel destroyed him in two or three minutes.

'You say, Professor, if I have understood you correctly, that the accused is a psychopath, that psychopathy is a congenital condition, and that therefore his responsibility is diminished?'

'Yes, that is correct.'

'What is the evidence that he is a psychopath?'

'His crime was that of a psychopath.'

'Apart from his crime?'

The professor stalled and looked a little flustered that his word was being doubted. I realised that he had neither examined the papers in the case carefully nor examined the accused. There was no evidence that he had ever been violent before or had any of the defining characteristics of the psychopath.

After an embarrassing silence that seemed to last an eternity, during which I covered my eyes, counsel continued:

'There is no evidence, is there? What in effect you are saying is that we know that he is a psychopath because of what he did, and he did it because he is a psychopath.' The professor uttered a sound that, thanks to his dry mouth and his confusion, was word-like without being quite a word.

'Thank you, Professor,' said counsel, with just the right hint of contempt.

The defence had one other expert witness in the case. He was a world-famous psychopharmacologist, also a professor, and a man of expansive presence and personality. He, too, strode confidently into the witness box. He wore a double-breasted navy chalk-stripe suit of the kind that only people of a type wear, and a bright yellow bow tie. Solicitors wear pin-stripes and barristers chalk-stripe — the back-room boys and the performers. They also wear different shoes. Solicitors who practice in criminal law pay no attention to their footwear, which is often cheap and scuffed, while that of barristers, even when only young and aspiring, is dear and brightly-polished. The professor had a barrel chest and a commanding manner: he would stand out in any company.

In his evidence-in-chief, the psychopharmacologist stated categorically that the accused must have been so drunk and uncoordinated from the pills he had taken, or rather said that he had taken, that he could not possibly have climbed the narrow stairs to the victim's room even the first time, let alone a second time after having drunk yet more alcohol and taken yet more pills.

'Let me be absolutely clear, Professor,' said prosecuting counsel. 'Your evidence is that the accused could not, for pharmacological reasons, have climbed the stairs?'

'Yes,' said the professor confidently.

'Thank you, Professor, no further questions.'

He left the witness box, the wings of his bow-tie flapping, as it were. I don't think, and certainly hope, that he had any idea what a fool he had been made to look: for he had stated that what the defence had already conceded had happened, could not have, and indeed had not, happened.

How and why was the stature of these two men, both brilliant in their field, so easily destroyed in the witness box by opposing counsel? For two reasons, the first being simply that they were such extremely busy men, constantly juggling the demands of administration with those of teaching, research, writing, speaking and travelling, that they had neither the time nor the inclination to master and commit to memory (even temporarily) the papers relating to a case that was, after all, a garden-variety murder and utterly without what Sherlock Holmes would have called 'points of interest.'

The second reason (I surmise) was that the professors had become too accustomed to their own eminence. It was for them to pontificate and for non-experts to believe without question.

I encountered the second of the professors, the psychopharmacologist, in another case. We met outside the courtroom before we were called. I took to him immediately. He was the kind of man one would like to have met at a dinner party, a fund of amusing, interesting and pointed stories, who clearly also had a keen enjoyment of the pleasures of the table. He was larger than life and better fun.

The case was that of a young man who had gone into a multi-storey car-park and there strangled a woman. Amazingly enough, he had done this out of the line of sight of CCTV cameras. Amazingly, for practically everything out of doors these days (at least in Britain) takes place on camera. One is a film star without knowing it.

The accused maintained that he was not and could not have been the killer because, on the day of the woman's death, he had been so intoxicated with cannabis that he could not physically have caused it. The professor, who was a world authority on the effects of cannabis, supported this defence — if, that is, the accused had taken as much cannabis that day as he said he had.

This time, I was called in to rebut the cross-examination evidence given by the psychopharmacologist. Prosecuting counsel had not challenged the professor's evidence directly in his cross examination. He had left that for me to do in rebuttal. The professor had, therefore, left the witness box with the air of a job well done. He did not wait to hear my response.

His evidence had been that the accused, a young ne'er-do-well, had smoked so much cannabis that he *must* have been physically unable to carry out a murder, if not actually unconscious.

A problem for this evidence was that there was a video of the accused walking in the street shortly before the murder was committed. The quality of the video was not good. I would not have recognised the man in it as having been the accused, but I was assured that the identity had been incontestably established. Having watched it, I said that, while it provided no evidence as to his fine coordination, it provided no evidence that he was as grossly uncoordinated as the professor said he must have been. The accused was walking as purposefully as any man might who had an appointment to keep. And it was for the defence to prove that he was incapably uncoordinated, not for the prosecution that he was not.

Furthermore, the professor's pharmacological evidence was, in my view, not only flawed but obviously flawed (even if the accused had smoked as much as he claimed, for which there was no evidence but his word for it, which was hardly disinterested). I pointed out that the concentration of the main active ingredient of cannabis varied greatly, by several-fold; that the quantity of smoke inhaled by the smoker varied greatly, by several-fold; and that the effect on the individual of the drug varied greatly, according to experience, expectations, circumstances, temperament and other factors; such that nothing whatever could be concluded about a man's conduct and state of mind merely from knowledge of the amount of cannabis he had smoked. Collateral evidence, therefore, was essential; and the man was convicted.

Another murder in a multi-storey car-park was the occasion of my meeting with a different type of expert, this time in forensic entomology, a discipline of whose existence I was until then unaware. He reminded me somewhat of the psychopharmacologist, though in fact he was far more self-deprecating, and his subject was insects, of course, rather than man. This murder was the denouement of a quarrel between two sellers of the *Big Issue*, the magazine founded to help the homeless help themselves, over territorial rights to sale pitches in the city. Nothing is important or unimportant but thinking something is makes it so.

I was waiting outside the court to testify and was joined

by a man with a splendid moustache. He, too, was in a chalk-striped suit. We fell to talking, and I asked him what he did.

'Oh,' he replied, 'I'm just a fly man.'

Much in the case depended upon the age of the corpse which, surprisingly, had remained undetected in the car-park for some considerable time. I have never been able, ever since this case, to enter or leave such a car-park without wondering where the corpse it might contain is hidden, even cast my eyes around for it.

The fly man, as he called himself, explained what I had only dimly apprehended before, that the species of maggots and other proofs of occupation by flies established, where circumambient conditions were taken into account, the likely age of a corpse. Flies colonise a corpse in an orderly and predictable succession of species, according to country, conditions, climate. The existence of a whole new world of erudition suddenly became evident to me.

The fly man explained his evidence to me with brilliant clarity and obvious authority, as well as love for his subject. He did so without condescension towards the ignorant, in this case me. While he spoke, the succession of species of fly inhabiting a corpse was the most important subject in the world. Yet at the same time he managed to convey that flies in a corpse were only one instance of the fascination and wonderment of the world. He was a man to whom I felt an immediate attachment.

He was called into court, too soon for me, who could have listened to him for years. I never met him again, but a few days later received a letter, via a newspaper, from Dr Zakaria Erzinclioglu, forensic entomologist, telling me how much he had enjoyed an article I had written and expressing his agreement with it. Forensic entomologists are not numerous, and I realised that the man I had met a few days earlier had been he.

I replied at once, of course, for there was no man with whom I would rather have become friends. But it was not to be. Shortly afterwards I opened the *Times* newspaper and my eye fell on the obituary of Dr Zakaria Erzinclioglu, who had died of a heart attack aged 50.

His trajectory had been unusual. Born in Hungary of Turkish parents, he had grown up in the Sudan and Egypt, studied zoology and entomology in Wolverhampton, and ended up in Cambridge. Unsuspected by me, who had not had a television for decades, he was becoming known as a television personality, presenting such programmes as *The Witness Was a Fly*. He knew how to slake a popular thirst for knowledge, and was the author of more than one book about murder and maggots, as well as an authoritative textbook on British blowflies (which is fascinating and oddly beautiful).

His obituary in the *Times* was written with unusual warmth, as if the author of it deeply and sincerely regretted the passing of Dr Erzinclioglu, and he succeeded in conveying that attractiveness of a person who could introduce himself as 'only a fly man.' Considering that I had met him only once and received but a single letter from him, I felt a surprisingly strong pang of grief on learning of his untimely death, a grief that I feel to this day when I recall him.

A few months after the *Big Issue* car-park murder and trial, as I was walking with my wife through the streets of the city, a seller of the magazine called out to me, 'Hello, doctor, do you remember me?'

I recognised though did not remember him. He had been a prisoner who had been under my medical care in the prison. I had examined him when he first came into prison.

'You wouldn't give me nothing for my heroin addiction,' he said. 'And you stopped all my pills.'

'Yes,' I replied, 'but I wouldn't have done it without explaining why.'

'Yes, but I thought you was 'ard, very 'ard.'

'It's always much quicker and easier to give the patient what he wants.' I said. 'It takes only a few seconds to write a prescription. An explanation takes much longer.'

'Anyway, I went to my cell after seen you and I thought on the way, 'I'll give it a try.' It was 'ard at first but it got easier. Now I've been off everything for a year and a half, the first time I haven't taken nothing since I was sixteen. And I haven't been in trouble since I came out.'

He was now thirty-two, living in a hostel and trying to make a little money by honest means for the first time in his life. He had been brought up in a children's home and had probably known little love or affection. His attempt to lead a better life was laudable and even impressive. At any rate, I was moved and of course bought a copy of the magazine from him, paying more than what he asked for it. He thanked me for what I had done for him — in truth very little — by denying him pills when it would have been easier to prescribe them and we shook hands. I wished him luck, but my words sounded hollow as I uttered them. A few words of encouragement against a lifetime of desolation, in a city and culture of desolation: how feeble they were.

It is easy to attribute success to oneself and failure to others. How was I to know whether I had really had the beneficial effect upon the seller of the *Big Issue* that he attributed to me?

The fact is that prisoners mature and by the time they are in their late thirties very few of them continue their life of crime, irrespective of what is done, or not done, for them. Perhaps my former patient, then, had merely been in the process of giving up crime anyway — after all, he decided to give abstinence from dugs a go — and my influence had been slight or non-existent. His biographic account was not enough for me to award myself retrospectively the role of redeemer.

2

Decision Time

Modern administration, such as in a prison, inevitably deals with classes of men, and not with men as individuals. I saw this in the way it dealt with a professional writer, an intelligent, sympathetic but far from sentimental man, who gave weekly writing classes to six prisoners who had expressed an interest in writing.

He told me that he had noticed a pattern among them. Almost inevitably their first efforts were autobiographical; they had no difficulty in relating the terrible childhoods that they had had. But then they came to a block in their narrative: and it was always at the point in it when they reached the commission of their first serious crime. The flow ceased; they could not continue. With what I imagine to have been great tact, however, the writer encouraged and coaxed them through their block, and eventually most of them were able to narrate their crimes. He himself managed unobtrusively to negotiate the narrow path between censoriousness and exculpation.

What was the origin of the block he described? I suspect that for the first time they thought biographically about their own lives, which forced them to confront the truth of what they had done, stripping away the excuses they had made for themselves. Yes, they had had terrible childhoods of cruelty or neglect; but still there was no inescapable, intrinsic, or simple causal connection between their experience and what they had done. In other words, they had *decided* to do what they had done, and writing their narrative forced them to confront this painful fact. I surmised that this confrontation with their own truth would hasten their abandonment of crime.

One day the writer came to me and told me that the funding for his work — he was not highly paid — was about to be withdrawn as an economy measure. He asked me for a letter of support, which I gladly wrote. Just as I had predicted, it had no effect. He came no more to the prison.

I can just imagine the official response to my letter of support. An administrator with all the right qualifications would declare to his colleagues that my support did not constitute 'scientific' evidence, that there were no statistics to show that writers reduced the rate of recidivism among prisoners, and that all policy and expenditure these days had to be 'evidence-based'.

Is such 'evidence' possible? The numbers in his writing group were tiny, not more than one in two hundred and fifty at any one time. Moreover, they were self-selected. They had volunteered for the class and it was unlikely that they were typical of prisoners as a whole as to age, character, intelligence, education and even criminal record. For any valid conclusion, all these factors, and no doubt others, would have to be taken into account. Moreover, the comparison would have to be between those who had applied to the writer and were accepted, and those who were refused (acceptance and refusal being allocated at random). It was obvious that such a comparison could not be made and would never be feasible — *ergo*, the writer should never be employed in the prison.

But if the writer once a year reduced the future time spent by a prisoner by a year, or even by six months, which is far from implausible, he would have earned several times his exiguous salary: at least if the annual cost of keeping someone in prison is to be believed (of course, the marginal saving on one individual prisoner might be nil, according to the calculations of scientific administration). It seemed to me a wager worth taking.

There was another argument in favour of retaining the writer, though not a convincing one in these Gradgrindian times. Though very far from a penological liberal — I think that many prison sentences should be far longer than they are — I nevertheless think that there is an ethical duty to try to do something for the prisoners, even if the efforts prove unsuccessful. The employment of the writer at least demonstrated that something, however small, was being attempted other than mere incapacitation. I favoured his classes, because it was my belief that the cultural world inhabited by the prisoners — their music, their electronic entertainment — reinforced, if it did not actually cause, their criminality.

Besides, there was an all too evident distinction made between the 'scientific' rigour with which the value of the writer's work was assessed, and the dubious standard which was used to assess that of the proliferating and vastly more expensive administrative procedures introduced almost daily into the service.

The assumption of modern bureaucracy is that new and expanded procedures are always better than the old; and even if this turns out to be indisputably false at some later stage, well — it is bureaucracy, not love, that means never having to say sorry.

New procedures mean new forms. These are invariably longer and more inclusive than the old, because more information is always better than less. Information-gathering is the process that will solve any problem, so that for every problem there is an apposite form. It doesn't exactly do anything about it, but it shows you have done something. Belief in forms is to us what belief in rain-makers was to African tribes subject to drought.

During my time, the Prison Service became worried about the numbers of suicides in prison — or rather about the publicity given to the numbers of suicides in prison at the time. It therefore decreed the use of a new form to be filled out on every prisoner thought by any member of staff to be suicidal or potentially suicidal.

The form was of such complexity that it would rarely be filled out correctly (which, as I shall explain, I came to see as its main virtue and purpose in the eyes of those who devised it). I recall being trained in its use by an officer who had himself been trained in its use and proselytised it with the zeal of a convert. The purpose of such zeal is to disguise the absurdity even from the convert himself. So it was in this case, for I knew the officer concerned to have been a perfectly reasonable, and even cynical, human being before his conversion. Give a man something absurd to do which he cannot avoid and he will soon become enthusiastic about it.

The form, many pages long, was soon used in more and more cases, for it was easier to open what soon became known as a 'book' on a prisoner than to close it, for negligence could never attach to 'opening a book,' but easily to closing one ('I've opened a book on Smith, Sir,' an officer would say to me, but never 'I've closed the book on Smith, Sir').

Thus prisoners 'on a book' proliferated until a high proportion were on one. Many years later, a naïve prison officer of African descent admitted in an investigation I conducted into the suicide of a prisoner that on his rounds he always looked first into the cells of those 'on a book,' just to check that there were no 'swingers'. 'That's what we call prisoners who hang themselves,' he said, 'swingers.' A British officer would have kept this locution to himself; the African demonstrated his lack of malice by doing so.

Much of the prison officers' time was now occupied by filling out these forms. There was, of course, no guarantee that they filled them honestly: if you can't trust a man to do his best, you can't trust him to follow procedure honestly. One suicide in the prison occurred, nonetheless, when there was a much reduced staff in the prison — everyone else was away at a 'suicide awareness training'.

Some time after the form was introduced, I was called to the coroner's court to give evidence on a prisoner who had hanged himself. Unlike other courts (in Britain), the coroner's court is inquisitorial rather than adversarial, but interested parties may be legally represented. The family of the deceased had retained a barrister in the hope of proving wrong-doing or negligence on the part of the prison, thus preparing the ground for eventual compensation — or 'compo' as it is known.

The deceased in question had not been well-liked by his family, who had not visited him in the three months of his imprisonment, though they lived only a short distance away.

I had not known him well and my connection with the case was slight. The barrister for the family, a young man, rose to question me. It was his aim to make the man's death everyone's fault but his own.

'It's true, isn't it, doctor,' he asked in a tone of menacingly unctuous politeness, 'the 20/52 SH [the designation of the form, SH standing for Self-Harm] was not filled out correctly?' The implication was that, if it had been filled out correctly, naturally the man would not have died.

'Yes, it is true,' I replied (though not actually knowing whether or not it had been filled incorrectly), 'but it is also true that the suicide rate in prisons has risen since its introduction.' That was the end of this line of questioning, and the barrister then asked me only one or two trivial and inoffensive questions just to avoid the impression of utter deflation.

The prison officers themselves were sceptical of the value of the forms they had to fill in, and there is no better way to reduce the moral of a staff than to impose upon it tasks which it believes to be meaningless but which are intricate and time-consuming. On the other hand, modern administration likes low morale, at least where its own direct financial interests are not concerned, because it makes staff resigned and therefore pliable.

One day a prison officer whom I found filling in the form asked me whether I would like to see where all the forms ended up.

He led me down into a labyrinth of subterranean corridors of whose existence I had previously been unaware. We came to a large room in which there were scores of metal stacks on which were placed huge transparent plastic sacks, each filled with hundreds of suicide forms, as they were sometimes known, and in which they had found their final resting places. The sacks were marked by indelible pen with dates: 'Jan — March 2001', for example. If any particular document had been needed, it would have been a Herculean task to find it.

'There!', said the officer, with all the disdain and contempt of which he was capable.

On the way back through the labyrinth, I was prey to a strange melancholy. Each of those thousands and thousands of forms represented considerable effort or labour. At what cost? To see them all stored higgledy-piggledy was a reminder of the myopia of modern administrators and the transience of existence.

I was called to the coroner's court in another case of suicide in prison. In my experience, for some reason that I cannot explain, coroners' juries always seemed to me more alert and better-dressed than juries in criminal trials. It cannot merely have been from a respect for death: juries in murder trials dressed no better than for those for lesser offences.

The man had hanged himself after ten days in prison and again I did not know him well. The witness before me, an administration-doctor in charge of the prison medical services for the whole area, had made a bad impression, being evasive, appearing to want to ensure that the blame, if any, fell on to the lowliest member of staff possible. The guilty flee where no man pursueth.

I had met the dead man only once, when I examined him immediately on his reception into the prison. He told me that he had been kicked by the police during and after his arrest and on examination I found clinical evidence of fractured ribs. I ordered an x-ray, telling him that it was not necessary from the point of view of treatment, but that it might provide evidence in case he wanted to make a complaint against the police. The x-ray showed nothing, but at post mortem fractures were found exactly where I had suspected them.

My evidence went well. I think the jury was favourably impressed that I had recorded the man's allegation, had asked for the x-ray and had in the end been proved right in my diagnosis. At the end of my evidence the coroner asked the jury whether it had any questions for me. The foreman, an intelligent-looking man in his later thirties, said he had a question.

'Why,' he asked, 'did the fractures not show on x-ray?'

'They often don't,' I said, 'if the ends of the fracture are not displaced. And muscular contraction would prevent them from becoming displaced.'

It sounded convincing and the jury was convinced.

But my appearance at coroner's court was not always so comfortable. In one case I was questioned by the mother of the deceased.

He was a man of about thirty who had long developed the strange habit of cutting his abdomen open and exposing his entrails (I had seen another such case nearly thirty years earlier in my career). He was also an habitual burglar. He was difficult to care for in prison and I warned him after he had cut himself open yet again that it would one day be impossible to close the wound and that he might die of septicaemia.

I knew that my warning would have no effect on his behaviour. A man who cuts his abdomen open repeatedly is not likely to be susceptible to a rational assessment of the likely consequences. He was not suicidal and expressed no wish to die, but he was prey to a strange compulsion that was stronger than the life instinct. To make matters worse, he was not an articulate man, able to explain, or rationalise, himself.

He returned from the hospital to prison one day having been treated surgically for his auto-laparotomy. I ordered that he be watched continuously through a gated cell: that is to say a cell without a solid metal door. He played with his wound, however, to prevent it from healing, and short of tying him up or sedating him to the point of unconsciousness there was little we could do to stop him.

I was on duty a couple of nights later when, at about ten o'clock, I was asked to attend to him. His wound was now oozing a considerable amount of blood. I could not see the source of the bleeding and he had already lost quite a lot of blood. I therefore sent him back to the hospital where he died about a month later of septicaemia.

The inquest into his death was presided over by a coroner against who I already had a slight grudge. He was a tall man, inclined to be fussy and pedantic (perhaps not altogether undesirable traits in a coroner), with a silly grey toothbrush moustache that somehow consorted well with his character.

On a previous occasion in his court I had described the number of patients I had to see in the prison in the time allotted to me. 'It sounds as if,' said the coroner, 'you don't spend very long with each patient.' This, of course, was the arithmetic truth, but he made it sound as if it were my fault, as if I had negligently created my own working conditions. I of course said nothing but I had not forgotten.

He allowed the mother of the dead man to question me. She was at once very aggrieved and aggressive. She said that no one, including me, had tried to help her son. (Though he had received every possible kind of therapy, from drugs to psychotherapy and cognitive-behavioural therapy. Nothing had made any difference.)

'You're a liar,' she screamed. 'You killed my son!'

The coroner allowed her to continue for some time in this vein, until she exhausted her admittedly limited repertoire of insults. He never reproved her or asked her to moderate her language. I wanted to reply: 'He was your son, you brought him up, no wonder he behaved as he did.' Of course I said no such thing.

In fact, the wellsprings of his conduct, as those of most complex human behaviour, remained an impenetrable mystery.

As I stepped down from the witness box, the court usher approached me.

'I think you'd better leave by the back entrance,' he said. 'We've had quite a bit of trouble lately with relatives attacking witnesses.'

I was shaken by this. Although I felt that I had done nothing wrong (the failure of a doctor's efforts is not in itself proof of wrongdoing, though the public is increasingly willing to take it as such), I left the court like a thief in the night.

What the usher had told me seemed to me of social significance. Why had the coroner permitted the dead man's mother to make allegations of so scurrilous a nature and insult me in public at the top of her voice? Her son had absorbed immense quantities of effort on his behalf. Correct to the point of punctiliousness himself, why did he demand no self-control of her? Was it kindness, compassion, cowardice or condescension?

I suppose he would have said that he allowed her to have her say, or scream, in court because her rage and grief would otherwise have remained unexpressed and therefore turned inwardly to fester, resulting in psychic damage and mental illness. This is to subscribe to the hydraulic view of human emotions, according to which any emotion which is not released outwardly builds up inside and eventually causes an explosion when it can be contained no more. Emotions, like liquids, are not compressible.

Whatever the truth of this view of human emotions, the fact that such emotional outbursts in court are accompanied by an increased rather than a decreased risk of violence suggests that it is not true.

The common understanding that different institutions or procedures have different functions has disappeared; they all now bathe in a tepid therapeutic broth, in which their first and inescapable purpose is to soothe the psyche of those who come into contact with them. The duty of care is the whole duty of mankind, for everyone is as fragile as a blown egg and may break into pieces at the very first requirement to comport himself in a restrained way.

The coroner seemed to have lost sight of the difference between an inquest and psychotherapy. It is also possible that the coroner, being obviously of upper middle-class social origin, felt that his authority over a woman of no education and lowly social origin was morally illegitimate and that, in view of her disadvantages, he had no right to demand of her any particular standard of behaviour.

If so, he would have felt that he had such a right only in the kind of egalitarian society that has never existed and never will exist. If my surmise is right there was something deeply condescending in his attitude: that there are types or classes of people which are incapable of decent and dignified public conduct.

I never took this attitude myself. I did not allow prisoners to swear in my consulting room, though I had no means (other than suasion) of preventing them from doing so. If a patient came to me and complained of 'a f…..g headache,' I would say:

'Hang on a moment. What's the difference between a headache and a f…..g headache?' It so happens that there is such a thing as post-coital headache, but this is not what he was complaining of. The patient would reply:

'That's the way I talk.'

'I know, that's what I'm complaining of.'

'Why should I change?'

'Well,' I replied, 'you wouldn't expect me to say to you, 'Here are some f…..g pills, take two of the f…ers every four f…..g hours and if they don't f…..g work, f…..g come back and I'll f.....g give you some other f...ers,' would you?'

The patient tended to agree.

No doubt there was a lot of disputable metaphysics in what I said, but it had its effect and in fact our relations would improve rather than deteriorate. One might even suggest that in using bad language he was testing me — whether I had belief in my own role in his life. If I did not I was the more easily manipulated or intimidated. The coroner's failure to control the mother of the dead man was a symptom of the decomposition of public culture.

I once witnessed a similar symptom in the criminal courts. I had been called in defence of a young man of sub-normal intelligence who had fondled a young woman at a railway station. The court had assembled and the clerk and the barristers were present. Next to me sat a couple of plain-clothes policemen. We were all waiting for the judge to enter. The victim's boyfriend, a malign-looking young man, was in the public gallery.

'I'll kill him when he gets out,' he said quite clearly for everyone to hear.

No one did anything. The accused heard it and was clearly terrified. He lived in a milieu in which such threats were not idle. The policemen looked at one another and then resumed their conversation in a low voice. The judge entered and the episode was forgotten — except perhaps by the accused.

In English law uttering a credible threat to kill is considered a serious offence. Yet right in the very heart of the criminal justice system a young man (in whom Lombroso would have had no difficulty in discerning criminal propensities) committed such an offence and got away with it without so much as a word of admonition. Everyone — including me — pretended that he had heard nothing in order to avoid the inconvenience of having to do something about it. All that is necessary for evil to triumph, as Burke is said to have said (but no one knows when or where), is for good men to do nothing.

3

Sticks and Stones

A prisoner about to be released told me that the first thing he would do when he got out was to kill his girlfriend, or rather his ex-, for in the course of his prison sentence (for assaulting her) she had written him what in prison parlance was called a 'Dear John', a letter from a girlfriend to a prisoner telling him that she was leaving him for someone else. Such letters usually read, 'Dear X, I love you and always will but I have waited too long and Dwayne from next door has moved in with me...'

Many of the prisoners emotions were strong and violent, but also shallow and fleeting. Their most durable ones were resentment and *amour proper* — a deep and abiding concern for themselves. The instability of their relations with women gave rise to jealousy, often insensate, for where there could be no presumption of fidelity there could be no trust. Promiscuity, sexual predation and the desire for the exclusive sexual possession of another are ill-assorted bed fellows. Arbitrary violence is a common way for jealous men to square the circle. It helps them (but only for a time, it is usually unsuccessful in the long run) to keep possession of a woman — it so preoccupied her with the problem of how to avoid the violence by discovering its causes that she had little time or energy for pursuing other men.

Often this particular prisoner ascribed his violence to brainstorms, a kind of epileptic phenomenon in the course of which he half-strangled the woman or pulled her across the room by her hair.

Oddly enough, the woman often accepted this explanation of his conduct, at least for a time. She thought that there must be something wrong with him because, in her words, 'his eyes just go.' The man, for his part, claimed to have 'lost it,' or 'gone into one,' the precise nature of 'it' and 'one' being unclear.

The woman agreed with the prisoner that he didn't know what he was doing. But a simple question disabused her of this idea: 'Would he do it in front of me?', I asked her. The scales fell from her eyes and she realised that his violence was more policy than impulse, and, more importantly, that she had been deceiving herself.

The prisoner who threatened to kill his girlfriend described himself as being in prison 'for her'. He made it sound as if, in assaulting her, he had conferred an inestimable benefit upon her.

What he meant, of course, was that she had informed against him. In similar fashion, when a mother once commented to me that she had a baby 'for' her boyfriend, current or ex-, that she was his 'baby-mother' and that he was her 'baby-father', there was no implication of any subsequent duty incumbent upon the boyfriend. That duty was the state's.

'Independence' for the mother was freedom from the father.

I asked the prisoner, when he threatened to kill his girlfriend, whether he meant it literally. He said that he did, and that he would go 'straight round hers' and kill her.

I had no choice but to notify the police, who soon arrived to question him. He admitted that he had uttered the threat and meant it. He was charged, tried and sentenced to five years' further imprisonment.

To this day, however, I am not sure whether this wasn't what he had wanted all along, preferring to stay in prison rather than recover his freedom. Early in my prison career I discovered something I had not in the least expected to find: that a surprising proportion of the prisoners preferred prison to life 'on the out'.

I have continued to wonder why it should have been so: for conditions in prison, while progressively less harsh, were still not such as would attract most people.

I was affected by a seeming paradox. In the morning I would see in the hospital next door the prison, in which I also worked, many patients who had been burgled, sometimes more than once or twice. In practically no case had the police caught the burglar, or even made any attempt to do so. So ineffectual were the police considered that sometimes the victims did not even bother to report the crime. It was pointless to do so other than for insurance purposes and many victims were too poor to take out insurance in any case. But in the afternoons and evenings, I would see many burglars who had been sent to prison that very day.

How to explain the paradox? I suspected that at least some of the burglars made themselves available for arrest, as it were. They wanted to be sent to prison.

After I started to wonder whether this was the case, I would take aside old lags (who were still, of course, young men) when they first entered prison for a new offence and ask them, in the strictest confidence, whether they preferred life in prison to life outside. Many would admit that they did, at least for a time; and when I asked why, most of them replied that they felt 'safer' in prison than outside.

But safer from what?

In most cases it was from themselves. They did not know what to do with freedom and when a choice presented itself to them they always chose the most superficially attractive and most obviously self-destructive alternative. They caused chaos and misery around them, including to themselves, and were often under threat from the enemies that their own conduct provoked.

In prison, they had no choices to make, the routine was laid down for them, and life was not too arduous provided that they made themselves inconspicuous and gave the authorities no trouble. The wise prisoner called this 'getting his head down and doing his bird'. The prison had become for such types the rest-home of the underclass.

Another advantage for them of prison was that there were no women, apart from an increasing number of female officers. No mother of their offspring badgered them for money for the kids' shoes (it always seemed to be shoes that money was needed for), and there was no angry ex- or future boyfriend of the woman in their lives to worry about. For them, prison was not necessarily to be feared.

One day I asked one of my patients, who had just come

from being sentenced and who appeared deeply upset, what he had got.

'Three months,' he said angrily.

'Three months,' I repeated. 'Isn't that a good result?'

In prisoner's parlance, a 'good result' is a sentence shorter than expected.

'Three months is no use to me,' he said, still angry. 'I was hoping for at least twelve.'

In a large number of cases, prison was quite literally a health-farm. It was the only place in which prisoners sought or received any medical care. Though overwhelmingly young men who should have been at the peak of condition, they were frequently very unwell or suffering from injuries when they arrived in prison. At one time I considered writing a spoof medical paper titled 'Injuries of Attempted Escape from the Police'. A number of them would arrive with bramble scratches all over them: they had rushed into the nearest brambles in an attempt to shake off their pursuers. It was only after I noticed these scratches that I noticed also what I had previously seen but failed to observe, namely that there were brambles on patches of waste ground in the city — whose fruit, incidentally, though a free gift of nature, no one in the area, though invariably poor, bothered to collect, perhaps because most people had lost altogether the habit of making food for themselves, eating nothing that had not been industrially-processed.

The heroin addicts were in a particularly parlous state when they arrived in prison. They often had thrombosed (blocked) veins in their arms. Looking for a functional vein, they progressed from arms to groin, to ankle, to neck, always in that order, and on one occasion I met an addict who had experimented with his eye as a portal of entry of heroin into his body.

The addicts would be so emaciated that they could have served as extras in any film made about a concentration camp. After a few months inside, they would look a picture of health again. Alas, they would return a few months after their release in the same cadaverous condition. Some of them had even begged the magistrates or judges to send them to prison so that they could get 'clean' again, as they called it, that is to say free of drugs. But the desire to get clean was not the same as the will-power to resist the temptation of drugs once they were released.

It was because of my work in the prison that I came to doubt what might be called the official view of heroin addiction, namely that it is a disease ('a chronic relapsing brain disease', according to the American National Institute on Drug Abuse) like any other.

Prisoners who had just arrived in prison were kept in a waiting room before they came, one by one, to be examined by the doctor. Unbeknown to them, I would often watch them in the waiting room before starting my examinations. They were animated, laughing and joking among themselves. But as soon as they entered my room they doubled up in pain, allegedly suffering withdrawal effects from heroin.

'I'm clucking,' they would say, or 'I'm doing my cluck.'

They meant that they were going cold turkey, one of the effects of withdrawal being contraction of the smooth muscle of the hair follicles, giving to the skin an appearance of plucked poultry. Turkeys, of course, gobble rather than cluck, but 'I'm gobbling' or 'I'm doing my gobble' doesn't have quite the same elegant expressive ring to it as 'I'm clucking' or 'I'm doing my cluck.' On the other hand, neither does 'I'm going cold chicken' have the same elegance as 'I'm going cold turkey.' Sometimes a mixed metaphor is best.

Doubling up in pain implied abdominal cramps, another symptom of withdrawal.

'It's strange,' I said. 'You seemed all right a moment ago when I watched you in the waiting room.'

Some of them would straighten up, laugh and say, 'Well, it was worth a try.' Others would claim that I could not know how serious their condition was because I'd never had it.

'I've never had cerebral malaria or cancer of the bowel either,' I said, 'but I know it's serious.'

The addicts were trying to obtain sedatives, or better still opioids, from me. When they realised that the game was up, that I was not to be duped, some took it well and others with the fury of the justly-accused.

My reassurance that they would be checked regularly for signs of withdrawal and given relieving medicine if necessary did not placate all of them, of course. Pill in the hand was worth two on the morrow. In addition, pills, of whatever kind, were the local currency in the prison and could be used to buy what few possessions other prisoners had. In an enclosed world, the smallest distinction, privilege or possession becomes huge.

In practice, I never saw any serious consequences of heroin withdrawal — not one in hundreds of cases. The dramatic depictions in books and films are gross exaggerations. But the tradition is now so firmly rooted that it is seemingly ineradicable; literature and the cinema have struggled with pharmacological truth and emerged triumphant. When I tell laymen, and even some doctors, that withdrawal from heroin is not serious, let alone dangerous, they find it difficult to believe me. The horror of cold turkey is an article of modern humanity's faith.

By contrast, withdrawal from alcohol can be very serious and in some cases, if untreated, fatal. If on arrival in prison an alcoholic seemed likely to suffer from withdrawal, I would prescribe him sedation prophylactically to prevent the development of serious and dangerous symptoms.

Oddly enough, however, alcoholics in contrast to the drug addicts never tried to inveigle medication from me, nor even asked for it when it was necessary. And another oddity was that the Prison Service (and Home Office) was much exercised by the treatment of withdrawing drug addicts, and not at all by that of withdrawing alcoholics, though *delirium tremens* untreated has a death rate of between five and ten per cent. Concentration on the trivial (or is it publicity?) at the expense of the serious is the mark of a modern bureaucracy.

I also discovered — or rather, came to know what others had discovered — that the relationship between crime and heroin was not as straightforward as commonly supposed.

Most heroin addicts who were sent to prison had long criminal records, well before they ever took heroin. For most of them, imprisonment came before heroin; most of those imprisoned had been convicted five or ten times before their first imprisonment; and most of those told me in confidence that they had committed five to twenty times as many offences as they had ever been charged with.

It followed that many if not most had committed between twenty five and two hundred crimes before they ever took heroin, so the need to 'feed their habit,' as they called it, could not have been the whole explanation of their criminality. At most it reinforced their criminality. In so far as there was a causative relationship between heroin and criminality, it was as much that the latter caused the former as the other way round. More probably, whatever attracted them to a life of crime equally attracted them to heroin.

I thought it important that the addict should not deprive himself of agency while conferring it on an inanimate substance. Injecting addicts take heroin irregularly on average for eighteen months before becoming physically addicted to it. Moreover, an injecting addict has much to learn, for example how to prepare the drug and how to inject it. They have to overcome a natural inhibition against sticking a needle in oneself. Moreover, they know the consequences of addiction, for most of them come from areas where addiction is common.

Not only the heroin addicts, but many other prisoners sought medication from the doctor as soon as they arrived in prison. I remember a man who asked whether I would give him diazepam, a tranquilliser much valued and sought after in the prison.

'No,' I said.

'No?' he repeated, 'What do you mean, no?'

'I'm very sorry,' I said, 'I really can't think of a simpler way to put it.'

I explained my reasons for not prescribing it despite the fact that withdrawal from diazepam can lead to epileptic fits and (very rarely) to something like *delirium tremens*. My explanation did not impress the prisoner.

'Murderer!' he exclaimed. 'You're not a doctor, you're a murderer!' Then he stood up and shouted 'Murderer! Murderer! Murderer!'

As we were then in the old Victorian part of the prison, with large spaces and much wrought ironwork, his voice echoed and reverberated round the whole prison.

'That's enough,' I said. 'You can go.'

Two officers escorted him away, while he turned his head in my direction shouting, 'Murderer!'

The prisoners who followed him for examination were as little lambs. They demanded nothing and I was able to prescribe for them only what I thought they needed, without any complaint or protestation on their part.

I was walking through the prison next day when I came across the prisoner who had called me a murderer the day before.

'I'm sorry about last night, doctor,' he said. 'I was bang out of order.'

'Oh, don't worry about it,' I said. 'It doesn't matter.'

'No, but I shouldn't've called you a murderer.'

'I've been called worse.'

'Anyway, I'm sorry.'

'Actually,' I said, 'you had a wonderful effect on the other prisoners. I've never seen them so calm and well-behaved as they were afterwards. You couldn't come and do the same thing again tonight, could you?'

We parted on good terms. My slight anxiety that he might actually have needed diazepam to avoid withdrawal was allayed. He had only been trying to 'blag' pills out of me. If I had prescribed them, he would have thought me a fool.

A very high proportion of prisoners were taking psychotropic drugs of one kind or another when they arrived in prison. This was not because they needed them or because the pills did them any good medically, but because GPs and specialists didn't know how otherwise than by prescribing they should respond to their demand for pills. Many of them were the type of patients who, if they did not get what they wanted, became threatening, and doctors outside prison did not have prison officers to help them prescribe only according to the strictest medical indications.

The prisoners' attitude to pills was odd.

If they found them they took them without the slightest knowledge of what they were or what their effects would be. What they wanted was a change in their state of mind. They wanted to feel different, not necessarily better.

A change was as good as a cure. Two prisoners sharing a cell came across a cache of white pills left by the previous occupant, an epileptic who had not taken his medication as prescribed. They shared the pills between them and took them all at once. They soon became dizzy, nauseated and uncoordinated, and had to be sent to hospital.

The previous occupant, the epileptic, had not taken the pills because he preferred to have an epileptic fit now and again, after which he would be sent to hospital where his girlfriend would be allowed to visit him whenever she felt like it. It was also a break from the monotony of prison life.

Being sent to an outside hospital — the prison had a hospital wing of its own — had another advantage for some prisoners. It was far easier to escape from it than from prison. Indeed, the only escapes from the prison in the fifteen years I worked there were from the outside hospital.

At the beginning of those fifteen years, the patient-prisoners were still chained to their bed, but this was thought degrading and the chains were removed. This made successful escape very promising, especially if they were treated on the ground floor. The only prisoner who tried to escape from a higher floor slipped as he ran down the stairs barefoot and broke his ankle, necessitating an operation.

At least two prisoners escaped from the ground floor. One of them was as slender as a ferret and managed to squeeze out of the lavatory window, this having previously been certified as impossible by the prison's security department. Another prisoner, feigning an unconsciousness that was plausible in view of his medical condition, lulled the two guarding officers by his bed into a false sense of security and then suddenly leapt up and dived head first through the window above his bed. He managed to get clean away, though he must have been conspicuous in his hospital robe as he ran through the streets.

In both cases, the escapees returned to their last known address, where they were almost immediately arrested.

In one of those semantic shifts that reveals much about the way we live now, the word 'abuse' has been replaced in the parlance of doctors and others who 'treat' addicts by the word 'use'. A prisoner complained to me one evening of symptoms in his chest. He was an armed robber of banks. Examination revealed nothing and his symptoms were not those of any condition known to me. They made no medical sense.

But in the past the prisoner had suffered from both lung abscesses and pulmonary embolus, serious and life-threatening complications of his intravenous drug abuse. I decided to send him to the hospital next door for further tests just to be on the safe side.

After I had made my decision the duty governor came to see me.

'Is it really necessary to send him out to hospital tonight doctor?' he asked.

'Well,' I replied, 'the only condition that could pose an immediate threat to his life (*pulmonary embolus*) could be treated in prison until tomorrow and he could be sent out tomorrow.'

'You see, doctor,' he said, 'we've had intelligence that his mates are going to spring him from the hospital.'

'In that case,' I said, 'I'll arrange for him to be seen in a different hospital.'

It would have been interesting to know how this 'intelligence' had been gathered: no doubt there was involved some murky — though necessary — connection between the worlds of crime and criminal justice. But it was not my place to ask. Though by then I had worked many years in the prison, there was much that went on of which I had no idea. But if I had said to the governor that the prisoner needed to be sent to hospital there and then, he would have arranged it, however inconvenient it might have been for him to do so, for he trusted my judgment.

The intelligence was confirmed the following day in an unexpected manner. The prisoner went off to hospital in an ambulance and when he realised that he was not being taken to the hospital in which his friends were waiting for him, he demanded that the ambulance turn round and take him back to prison. As far as he was concerned, there was no further point in going to hospital; but the inexorable rule, to his irritation, was that an ambulance could not be deflected from its destination once it had started out for it.

4

Prison Officers

'Reprimanded more likely'

Suicide remained a serious problem among prisoners — as it was, with much less publicity, among prison officers who, in an attempt to raise their status, had long since ceased to be called warders. I recall my first encounter with the Senior Medical Officer in the prison in which I was to spend a longer time than many a robber. I had gone to visit a patient of mine from the hospital next door who was later imprisoned. I found the SMO (as he was known) sitting at his desk with his head in his hands, a volume of Schopenhauer before him.

'What's the matter, Dr S?' I asked him.

'We've just had a suicide,' he replied. 'I don't know what's worse, the suicide or the forms we have to fill in afterwards.'

One might have thought that Schopenhauer developed his sense of humour in prison. Some people, in order to maintain their reputation in their own minds for virtue, would feel shocked or offended by this seeming callousness, having lost the awareness that irony is a necessary defence against tragedy.

In fact, I had known Dr S from another prison where I had worked for a few weeks as a stand-in for a friend, and where he had been SMO before he was transferred to this much larger prison. He knew me to be reasonably reliable and competent from these weeks and asked me whether I would like to work in the prison. I said that I would, and thus began my fifteen years of service, for fourteen of which I was on duty one night and one weekend in three or four.

I did not realise then that this was the end of an era (who does realise such a thing?) in which anyone could be recruited in so informal a manner, a manner ripe with possibilities for corruption, nepotism and back-scratching, but at the same time so simple and efficient. It implied a trust in the judgment of the person who hired, without the intermediation of a process, supposedly perfectly fair, many components of which were both time-consuming and doubtfully-related to the recruit's ability to do the job. The SMO knew me, I was good enough, I started to work.

I liked and respected the SMO. He was a man of independent judgment, unafraid to go his own way. He taught me a very valuable lesson about how to deal with modern management.

One day he showed me a form sent to him by the Home Office about the prison's needle exchange scheme. We had decided between us that we were not going to mount such a scheme in our prison, whereby injecting addicts would be able to exchange old needles for new, the sharing of needles being the means of spread of viruses such as Hepatitis C (a cause of later cirrhosis and cancer of the liver) and HIV (the cause of AIDS). Our decision not to implement official policy was not unreflective. Although we had had hundreds of prisoners who had injected, we had never had an overdose of heroin in the prison or found any discarded needles or syringes as we would have done had the addicts continued to inject while in prison. The SMO and I therefore decided against what might be called anticipatory appeasement.

The SMO picked up the Home Office form and held it up between his thumb and forefinger as if it had been some kind of struggling noxious insect and then dropped it into the waste-paper basket beside him.

'If I so much as put a mark on that paper and send it back,' he said, 'I'll never hear the end of it. But if I just throw it away, all that will happen is that they will send another one in six months.'

He was quite right, of course. This went on for several years, the computer dutifully generating another form every six months.

The SMO was not much involved in clinical work. It is quite common, increasingly so, for doctors, once they have reached a certain age and seniority, to feel that they have seen enough patients in their life and to retire into administration. Nevertheless, the SMO would attend my ward rounds in the hospital wing. He would sit at a desk beside me but I would do all the talking and examining. The patients, mostly ambulant, were bought in one by one.

As the ward rounds took place after lunch, Dr S was often rather sleepy and indeed did tend to nod off. Once he was sleeping peacefully when a patient was brought in who believed that he was Jesus. Religious delusions were once common but with the decline in religious belief delusions tend to attach to other subject matters.

The young man who thought he was Jesus was quite

excitable, and he was frustrated that no one would believe him. His imprisonment, to him, was part of his martyrdom.

'How do you know you're Jesus?' I asked him.

'My father, which art in Heaven, hath told me,' he said, employing language that is not often heard in prison. He banged the table with his fist, which woke Dr S with a start.

'And your mother?', I asked.

'Oh, she lives in South Shields.'

I managed to keep a straight face. And after all, why should not the Mother of God live in South Shields? Would God not choose it rather than, say, Aspen, Colorado, where they have less need for such events, and illustrating what liberation theologians used to call the 'preferential option for the poor'?

At first, when I came to work in the prison the officers were wary of me, as a kind of foreign interloper. They assumed, until proved otherwise, that every educated person took the part of the prisoners against the prison, more or less *ex officio*, because they feel the need to carry their compassion for the poor and downtrodden with them.

I was not one of these, but I was aware of the need to retain my independence of judgement in each and every case and not to become totally identified with the team in so all-embracing an institution such as the prison. Prisoners obviously lied and cheated, wheedled and cajoled, but that did not mean that they could not stand in need of consolation or fall dangerously ill.

The common view of prison officers, is that they are uneducated men (and women) of sadistic inclination who enjoy exercising unbridled power over those entrusted to them by the state. And it would be useless to deny that there were a few among them who fitted this description, or that the opportunity to do evil with impunity in such an institution was unusually great.

But the majority were not like this. They were not, on the whole, highly educated of course. But that did not mean that they were senseless, as some who are proud of their education might think. They showed a practical understanding of the people in their charge which was shrewd, intelligent and penetrating and not lightly to be disregarded.

I saw many more acts of kindness than of sadism and I found that, on the whole, they were better observers of men than psychiatric nurses because their minds had not been filled with rigid theories that distorted their perceptions.

The officers had a camaraderie which arose from and soothed their peculiar situation. They were, in a way, as much prisoners as the prisoners themselves. They could be moved from one part of the country to another at very little notice and without any say in the matter, as could the prisoners, but when they arrived in their new post they would find conditions and social life very much like those they had just left. Work in what the American sociologist, Erving Goffman, called 'total institutions', that are a world unto themselves, such as the army, boarding schools, prisons and mental asylums, has its compensations — *esprit de corps*, a ready-made social life, a feeling of purpose, and even a sense of superiority to the rest of the world which knows nothing of life inside them.

Officers still maintained the (to me) pleasant custom of addressing each other always as Mr Smith or Mr Jones, at least inside the prison, and never by their first names, even if they were on very friendly terms. By contrast, they called the prisoners by their surnames, Smith or Jones, until the order came on high that they should also be called Mister. I should not have minded this had not the orders in the hospital next door been precisely the opposite, namely that Mr Smith and Mr Jones were henceforth to be addressed by their first names, or even diminutives of the first names such as Bill and Jack, supposedly on the grounds that it was friendlier. Thus, while patients were to be infantilised, prisoners were to be specially respected. The dystopian reversal of crime and illness was precisely like the one in Samuel Butler's *Erewhon*.

The officers' humour was of the distinctly gallows variety. In the days of capital punishment, that expression was not merely metaphorical. (It was said — though the story must be apocryphal, for it could not really have happened — that a prisoner on his way to what was known as 'the topping shed' remarked to the officers who accompanied him that the weather wasn't very nice. 'It's all right for you,' said one of the officers, 'you're not coming back.')

One day a prisoner arrived who had many piercings. Tattoos and other forms of decorative self-mutilation are statistically associated with criminality, and have been for a long time: Lombroso remarked on it a century and a quarter ago. More than ninety per cent of white British prisoners are tattooed (only smoking is more common among them), though the nature of the tattoos changed over the fifteen year period that I was at the prison.

At first the tattoos were predominantly amateur, monochrome in India ink. They were either self-inflicted or done by an associate, often in the prison itself (where it was considered an offence) by an associate with no special skill. They would consist of a few words — for example, 'Made in England' around a nipple, or 'LOVE' and 'HATE' on the dorsum of the fingers of both hands. The favourite initials tattooed were 'ACAB', which stood for the words 'All Coppers Are Bastards', unless the bearer happened to be taken to the police station, where they stood for 'Always Carry A Bible'. Occasionally I saw a crude tattooed picture of a policeman hanging from a lamp-post on a forearm, which I should imagine was not an asset to a man under arrest. 'LTFC' and 'ESUK' were other initials tattooed on the backs of fingers, which when put together read 'lets fuck'. This was shown to women in a pub, and I asked the men who bore these letters whether this method of seduction ever worked. Sometimes, they replied; and when it did, it made the whole effort worthwhile.

Another favourite design of cottage-industry tattooing was a dotted line around the neck or wrist with the words 'CUT HERE', in the more elaborate cases with a picture of a pair of scissors. 'NO FEAR' in large blue letters on the side of the neck was another favourite, often of small or slight men who would count for nothing in a social world whose hierarchy was decided by violence. Unfortunately, the words were often taken as a challenge rather than as a warning and those who bore them were sometimes attacked for no other reason, one of my patients having suffered a fractured skull as a remote consequence of his tattoo.

More recently, tattooing has become more widely fashionable, ascending the social scale faster than any social climber ever managed. And prisoners, following the fashion (assuming it was not they who set it), from the crude India ink variety to the elaborate multi-coloured 'body-art' variety of the professional tattooist. Oddly enough, the designs of most of this art strongly resemble those of the prisoners when they begin to draw or paint in prison, such that the criminal kitsch aesthetic seems to have spread though society.

The new body art tells us something about the emotional life of prisoners. They have the names of their girlfriends tattooed on their arms, for example, and usually in conjunction with a heart and foliage and pierced by an arrow, as a sign of their undying devotion to her. Alas, undying devotion often dies, to be replaced by a longer-lasting emotion, namely hatred. The name of the formerly beloved is then incorporated into another tattoo rendering it almost illegible, or in some cases is merely eradicated by crossed lines. As for paternal duty, it is demonstrated — and could it go further? — by the inscription of the names of the children, usually on the outer aspect of the upper arm. Increasingly prisoners with darker skins were tattooed as well, in imitation of their white peers, though a dark skin is not favourable to tattooing. Here was a fine example of integration or acculturation.

But to return to the prisoner of many piercings. The Home Office had decreed that every prisoner was entitled to one piercing but not more. It did not legislate for the part of the body in which that one piercing had to be: that was left to the prisoner to decide. 'If I had my way, sir,' said an officer on the arrival of the multi-pierced prisoner, 'I'd 'ang 'em all up by their earrings.' Prison officers often expressed opinions that would horrify those (increasingly many) who think that everything means exactly wat it appears literally to mean. Another officer, on the verge of retirement, said to me that they, the prisoners, should be given nothing three times a day, and plenty of it.

Notwithstanding these expressions of contempt for those under their care, most officers were devoted to duty to the point of willingness to risk their lives to save those of prisoners. A new hospital wing had been built at enormous expense in the prison, but it was typical of modern architects that, unlike the Victorians, he who designed it failed to consider the problem of ventilation in the event of fire. One day soon after the new wing had opened, an excitable prisoner set fire to the mattress in his cell. It seemed that years of research had gone into the disproof of the old saw there is no smoke without fire, and finally a mattress had been developed that, when lighted, would emit dense black smoke without flame. It was smoke of the kind that battleships used to emit to screen themselves from the view of pursuers.

Acrid black smoke began to seep from under the locked door of the prisoner's cell. Seeing this, an officer rushed to open it. A cloud of black smoke billowed out, and the officer rushed into the cell to pull the prisoner to safety. In doing so he probably saved the prisoner's life.

I arrived on the scene immediately afterwards. The prisoner was suffering from smoke inhalation, as was the officer to a lesser extent. While they waited for the ambulance to take them to hospital I praised the officer for his heroism and said that I supposed he would receive a commendation from the governor. By nature a quiet and reserved man, he replied only with a wry smile.

He returned to work a couple of days later. I asked him whether the governor had commended him yet.

'Reprimanded, more likely,' he said.

'What?' I said, genuinely amazed. 'But you saved a man's life!'

'Yes,' he said, 'but I didn't follow procedure.'

The proper procedure, apparently, the failure to follow which was worthy of a reprimand, would have been to have called the fire brigade and to have waited for it to arrive. Maybe the man would have died as a result, but at least the proper procedure would have been followed. Here is modern administration in its *reductio ad absurdum*: so afraid to leave any initiative to workers because they might make a mistake or exercise their own intelligence that it prefers its own rules to be followed to their direst consequences.

The officer was duly reprimanded and a black mark (for disobedience) was put on his record for having saved a prisoner's life in the wrong way, that is to say at risk to himself. But I knew the man: if he had to do it again, he would. Some years later, after I had stopped working for the prison service but was doing medical-legal work, I was asked to investigate a hanging in prison. Asked why he had not rushed into a man's cell to cut him down, an officer replied, 'I could lose my job for saving a man's life.'

Thanks to the design of the new wing, it took days for the smoke in the cell to disperse. It was as if it had been designed with the object of suffocation of prisoners in mind; as something to be promoted rather than avoided. In the Victorian part of the prison, the smoke would have dispersed at once.

Prison officers had often to face things that few of us ever have to face, let alone accept. It is true that some prisoners greet prison officers like long-lost friends when they return for the umpteenth time to the 'Big House', but others exhibited an implacable hostility towards them and insulted them horribly. Rarely did they retaliate in kind and I have several times witnessed officers being spat at full in the face without becoming violent in turn. On the vast majority of occasions they showed admirable self-control such as few of us are called upon to show, at least not repeatedly and almost every day.

A prison officer who had retired after many years' service found that he missed the work and returned part-time afterwards. Soon after he did so, members of two rival gangs of drug-dealers started a fight on the exercise yard. (With the grandiose delusion of such types, they called their struggle a 'war'.) Officers rushed in to break it up, among whom was the retired officer. In the melee, he was kicked and punched and was quite badly bruised. He was off work for a couple of days and then returned. His attitude was very different from those who use the most trifling medical excuse to avoid work. I remarked to him how surprised I was to see him back so soon, and his reply has stuck in my mind as an example of modest stoicism. 'I've been injured three times in thirty years,' he said. 'I don't call that bad, do you, doctor?'

Of course, I don't want to make officers into plaster saints: and they themselves would not want such an absurd depiction. They were often hard-drinking men and would not claim for themselves any great refinement. Furthermore, as I have mentioned, when they were bad they were very bad.

Prison officers and such men were difficult to dismiss for two reasons. First, when they behaved badly, they did so in secret. Modern employment law makes it difficult to sack someone on a mere suspicion, however strong it may be; proof of wrongdoing is necessary. Second, defence of one of their own was very important to prison officers.

There was among them, for example, a bully whom we strongly suspected of tampering with the emergency equipment for resuscitation. Every time the equipment was inspected or used, a small but important piece of equipment was missing, though we knew it had been replaced in the meantime. In other words, a member of staff — we assumed it was the same one — had removed it, presumably with the object of causing attempts at resuscitation to fail. The sheer malice of this hardly needs to be pointed out. (Several years later, preparing a report on a prison death, I came across a similar phenomenon in a prison two hundred miles away. It could not have been the same man, who in the meantime had retired.)

A second officer was even worse — assuming the tamperer with the equipment was always the same man. He had trained as a nurse and was therefore deployed in the hospital wing. The dual training, as prison officer and nurse, gave him additional opportunities for sadistic practices.

Once I was visiting a prisoner in a cell with him accompanying me. As we arrived, the prisoner fell to the floor and had an epileptic fit.

'Don't you do that in front of the doctor,' said the nurse severely to the unconscious, jerking figure on the ground.

'Actually, officer,' I said to him, 'he's having an epileptic fit.'

Some time later, a prisoner had a severe chemical injury to his eye, which blinded him in that eye. The nurse-officer was suspected of having infused it with a noxious chemical; but the victim refused to testify against him for fear of retaliation. I think that the fear was unjustified — in such a case, not even his brother-officers would have defended him — but I understood it.

Later the officer was dismissed for some repeated administrative infraction, always easier to prove than serious wrongdoing. Thus the ostensible aim of employment regulations, perfect justice, produces something very different, likewise the proliferating bureaucratic regulations aimed at improvement.

5

The Money of Frauds

The prison changed in the fifteen years I worked in it, mostly for the better. I arrived not long after integral lavatories had been installed in every cell: until then, there had been the daily practice called 'slopping out', the emptying of a bucket provided for the calls of nature during the night. It now seems incredible to me that such conditions should have persisted into the 1980s with hardly any protest.

I am not one of those who thinks that prison conditions should be so hard that they in themselves act as a deterrent, though I am by no means a penological liberal either. Brutish conditions call forth brutality in those who administer them. What counts as brutal evolves with time — what is deprivation today would have counted as luxury in the past. Besides, punishment is not automatically justified by its efficacy. No doubt the public execution of people who park on double yellow lines would discourage such parking, but few — I imagine — would be in favour of it.

The improvement in conditions was mainly physical. By

the time I retired, the cells in the modern part of the prison had reached the level of comfort of rooms in the chains of cheap hotels.

No doubt some find this shocking, but I do not. I remember as a medical student in the early 1970s being taken with other medical students on a tour of a prison. We were accompanied by a group of magistrates. The conditions in those days were truly grim. The tour included the kitchens and one of the magistrates declared himself so impressed by the food that he said he wouldn't have minded a spell in the prison himself. This remark disgusted me, and it disgusts me still in recollection of it.

For me the main horror of prison would be the lack of privacy, the forced promiscuity of social (or antisocial) intercourse with others not of one's choosing, social intercourse without the possibility of trust or true friendship. If by chance friendship formed, it would soon be lost for prisoners are moved around like pieces on a board game by an unseen but all-powerful player.

And in any case, I fear forced intimacy far more than I fear solitude; as for the deprivation of liberty, it is the subjection to arbitrary and frequently stupid or irrational orders that I would hate more than an inability to leave the place. I think, however, that I should retain an inner sense of freedom, for freedom is at least partially a matter of inner attitude as well as of external conditions.

The language of prison also changed while I worked there. When I arrived, for example, the expression 'the black aspirin' was still, just about, in use; but I never heard it in subsequent years. The black aspirin was the prison officer's boot, administered in a supposedly corrective fashion by a warder on a recalcitrant prisoner. 'In my opinion, sir', a prison officer would say to me, 'he needs the black aspirin.' The officer in question would never administer it, of course; and I did not point out that, from the purely pharmacological point of view, the term was inapt: it should really have been the black valium. Officers ceased to wear boots as part of their uniform.

Another expression that disappeared shortly after my arrival in the prison was 'the liquid cosh'. The liquid in question was chlorpromazine in syrup or suspension. Formerly used to treat the delusions and hallucinations of psychotic patients, it would render docile or even unconscious even the most refractory or belligerent person, and was often administered indiscriminately to prisoners mainly to keep them quiet — hence its sobriquet. Complaints about the abuse of it in this manner led to its almost total elimination from the prison pharmacopoeia: whereupon, of course, the old lags began to complain about its absence. They missed being liquid-coshed.

Two verbs also disappeared during my prison career: 'to PP9' and 'to mandarin'. They were similar in meaning. The PP9 was a large, rectangular battery that was used to power radios. Prisoners were allowed to buy them from their small monetary allowance or earnings in the prison workshops. No doubt the batteries were often used actually to power radios, but they were also used as weapons. Put in a sock, they could be wielded like the *bolas* of the Pampas cowboy to inflict a serious injury. Walking through the prison early in my career there, an officer asked me to see Jones. 'He's just been PP9ed.'

To be mandarined was to be hit in the same way, but with a tin of mandarin oranges that the prisoners were permitted to buy.

Prison argot, like all other argots, changes rapidly. I have Eric Partridge's magnificent dictionary of the language of prison and the criminal underworld published in the year of my birth, 1949, and hardly any of the expressions listed in hundreds of pages were familiar to me. Even so familiar and (I had assumed) an old expression as 'doing your bird' is not in the dictionary; and what might be called the sub-argot of drug addicts had changed completely in the meantime. There was no reference to needle and syringe as 'the works'; and nothing about 'track-marks', the line of inflammation of veins, usually up an arm, where the addict has injected himself.

I asked the staff not to use the lingo of addicts. When prisoners referred to 'the works', I said, 'You mean needle and syringe.' Track marks were *phlebitis*; 'shooting up' was injecting. When they said that they were 'hooked by heroin', I said, 'You mean you decided to take heroin regularly.' I had noticed that those who worked with addicts tend to adopt their language, nominally to appear friendly and uncensorious, the better to 'treat' them. But in reality it was because many of them admired the drug-addicted way of life which they had not the courage to follow themselves. Talking like them was the nearest they could come to it.

By contrast, I wanted to establish not so much distance, as the fact that I did not envy or admire what they did and how they lived, nor did I want to minimise the harm they were doing themselves. It never seemed correct to me that rejection or implicit criticism of a person's way of life necessarily was a rejection of his humanity. On the contrary, the ability to do wrong is if not *the* distinguishing characteristic of mankind, at least one such characteristic. The corollary of the sentimental view that to sympathise with someone you have to accept his worldview uncritically seems to me false and ultimately demeaning of him. No one can hold consistently to this total acceptance, in any case. There is, or ought to be, something beyond the pale for everyone.

I found that the prisoners had adopted a kind of psychobabble, no doubt a little later than it was adopted elsewhere. They would say that their 'head is a shed', that it 'needs sorting out', that their 'head's gone', and that when they acted violently, it was because 'I go into one'. Psychobabble might be defined as the use of confessional language in which nothing is confessed, a way of talking about oneself without revealing anything.

In addition to the inherent pleasure of talking about oneself, psychobabble has an auto-exonerating purpose. 'My head's gone,' for instance, suggests a physiological derangement that requires outside assistance to right, but no self-examination or control. The man with a 'gone' head is not asking for a Socratic dialogue to find out where he went wrong in losing it, but for a medical procedure, like the sewing back of a finger, or the prescription of a miracle drug that will 'sort out my head' as eggs are sorted into different sizes. Thus our addicts would say when they arrived in prison that they would stop taking the drug 'if only I got the help'. By help, they meant some technicality that would, by itself, without any resort to will-power, stop them from taking the drug.

It is a chimera assiduously peddled by a large professional apparatus of care, cheer-led by the American National Institute on Drug Abuse that defines addiction as a chronic relapsing brain disease, and as almost nothing else. Its somewhat ambiguous name is one which would suit almost as well an institute seeking to spread drug abuse as far and wide as possible.

When the addicts claimed to have been 'hooked' by heroin, as mentioned above, it was an evasion, if not an outright lie. The average injecting addict has spent many months taking the drug intermittently before becoming physically dependent on it, besides which he had to learn many things, such as where to obtain it, how to prepare it, and how to inject it. In other words, in the transaction between drug and a man, the man hooked the drug, not the other way round. Yet the purpose of the expression was encouraged and reinforced by the official doctrine of addiction as a brain disease and the need for medical treatment.

But how came they to be hooked by heroin?

When asked, they almost always replied, 'I fell in with the wrong crowd.' To this I would reply, 'Is it not strange that I meet many people who fell in with the wrong crowd, but no members of the wrong crowd itself?' They would always laugh, grasping the point immediately. I had revealed to them something that they had always known (as Dr Johnson said, we need more often to be reminded than informed): that they had joined the wrong crowd by elective affinity and not by chance or by a force of social gravitation.

It was often said that prisoners were of lower than average intelligence, at least as measured by formal tests; but if so, I think this reflects more on the tests than on the prisoners, for I never found (except in the most obvious cases of mental deficiency, of whom there were very few) that I had to alter my way of speaking in order to be understood by them. It might be, I suppose, that what I was saying was itself of such a simple quality that it required no intelligence to understand it; but of course this is not my favoured explanation of the ability of prisoners to grasp what I said to them.

One prisoner on remand for a murder in a pub, described his crime as follows:

'A fight broke out, a gun arrived, I accidentally took it, and it went off.' The only human action that he admitted to was the accidental discharge of the gun, by happy chance killing an enemy.

The fight itself was an almost meteorological event, independent of anyone's will or choice, the result of atmospheric forces. No one *brought* the gun, it simply turned up under its own steam; it went off without anyone having wanted it to do so.

Did he seriously expect anyone to believe this preposterous account? Did he believe it himself? Was he whistling in the wind, or trying to gain my sympathy? I remember as a child being quite angry at having been accused of something that, in another part of my mind, as it were, I knew perfectly well that I had done, and done in the full knowledge that it was wrong. And yet my anger, at least as it must have been observed by others, was real enough; but I knew it to be *ersatz*.

There is no need for arcane psychoanalytic concepts or theories to explain this. It is the common experience of those who will, in the words of Dr Johnson (again) examine the motions of their own mind. To do this, however, there must be a Socratic interlocutor, either in one's own mind itself, or outside' and in this sense, the dialogues of Plato are infinitely more valuable than the case histories of Freud.

I often wondered which was the more immediately painful, to be justly or unjustly accused? I never quite resolved the question.

Anger could attach to both and it was impossible sometimes to distinguish between the true and false, the simulated from the real. There might also have been intermediate cases.

Once a very angry man, on remand for kidnap, came into my room and banged his fist on my desk. I asked him what was wrong and he told me that the police had just charged him with murder.

'I'm not a murderer,' he said vehemently. 'The police are trying to pin it on me and take away my character.'

He was so angry that I thought that it was possible that he was innocent. The innocent were, after all, sometimes both accused and convicted: not even the most scrupulous system of criminal justice could avoid such error altogether.

'The police are trying to take away my character,' he repeated. 'I'm not a murderer!' And he banged the desk again.

If it were a performance, it was a convincing one. To reduce his rage, knowing that he had already admitted to kidnap, I said mildly, in an attempt to lessen in his mind the iniquity of the police:

'But you are a kidnapper.'

Puzzlement overtook his rage.

'Well, yes,' he said, in the tone of, 'So what?'

'Kidnap is a serious crime, you know,' I continued as matter-of-factly as I could.

'Serious?'

'Yes, serious,' I said. 'You kept someone in a cupboard for three weeks.'

'I looked after him well.'

Immediately after his trial for murder, in which he pleaded guilty, he described exactly what he had done, in the most gruesome detail, to a prison officer, taking pleasure in the officer's repugnance.

Yet I had very nearly believed his protestations of innocence, and perhaps should have done so had I not asked him about the kidnapping to which he attached so little significance. I was by this time no longer the naïve and inexperienced person with regard to criminals that I had been when I started. A friend of mine, my mentor in prison medicine, told me of two experiences of his early in his career that illustrated the naïvety of a middle-class person confronted by the underbelly of his own society.

He had been a very young man when he conducted his first clinics in the prison. One day he said to an officer after a clinic, 'The prisoners didn't look a very nice lot today.'

'What you have to remember, Sir,' said the officer, 'is that they've all been in trouble with the police.'

Shortly afterwards, he finished another clinic and, having refused some of the prisoners the pills that they wanted, said to an officer that the prisoners did not look very happy. The officer drew himself up to attention, saluted, and said:

'That shows you're doing a good job, Sir!'

Questions of the guilt or innocence of prisoners

continued sometimes to worry me. Only a very small minority ever claimed to be totally innocent and in some cases their protestations were difficult to take seriously, for they had a long list of criminal convictions which they admitted. It was just *this* crime, the one for which they were imprisoned this time, that they had not done.

'I didn't do this one,' one said to me indignantly. 'It's a miscarriage of justice, that's what it is, a miscarriage of justice.'

I referred to the long list of previous convictions and he admitted that he had been guilty in those cases.

'I put my hands up to them,' he said. 'I done them. If I done this one, I'd put my hands up to it, but I didn't. It's a miscarriage of justice, that's what it is. The police fitted me up on this one.'

Again, his indignation seemed genuine enough, and I did not doubt that the police sometimes manufactured evidence in order to secure a conviction. They were humans, after all.

'Have you ever committed any crimes for which you were *not* caught?' I asked.

A smile came over the face of the prisoner as he recalled those happy occasions which were, in fact, many.

'Yes,' he said.

'And was there not a miscarriage of justice, then, in those cases?'

He did not reply.

'Try to think of his sentence as a punishment for them,' I said.

Of course, there was a slightly unscrupulous confusion, or conflation, in my argument between justice in the sense of a system of law and justice in a more Platonic sense, but whether or not he recognised it he did not object.

Like many prisoners, he had a child-like attitude to the state, as if it were, or ought to have been, an omniscient and omnipotent father and was shocked to discover that it had weaknesses and deficiencies. He became indignant over minor defects in a policemen's evidence against him, such as the precise time something happened, even where they did not affect the outcome or reflect in the slightest on their guilt or innocence. Such a defect more than abrogated the guilt of anything he had done. He was innocent because others were guilty.

I often asked prisoners who were on remand whether they were 'going' guilty or not guilty. They would usually answer, 'It depends.'

'On whether or not you did it?'

'On what my brief [my defence barrister] says.'

Guilt or innocence hardly came into it: the question was whether or not there was a realistic chance of acquittal.

In the abstract, at least, the systematic lighted sentencing of those who pleaded guilty at an early stage in the proceedings, and heavier sentences of those found guilty who maintain their innocence to the last, seemed to me unjust, almost a derogation of the right to a fair trial. It puts pressure on an accused to confess. And since there is rarely no evidence against an accused, even if innocent, he has to consider his chances irrespective of his guilt or innocence.

It turns justice into a game of poker, a question of who blinks first. A person who has been robbed or assaulted cannot be expected to think that an early confession weighs heavily in the balance against the original crime. It is true that the obstinate denial of guilt by the perpetrator may add somewhat to the distress of the victim, but the essence of a crime is its commission in the first place, not in its denial.

Even worse is plea-bargaining, according to which a man is charged with a serious crime and agrees (through his lawyer) to plead guilty to a lesser charge, to which the prosecution also agrees. Criminal justice should not be a souk in which merchant and customer haggle over a price to be paid. This is wrong in both directions. I have known lawyers encourage or persuade the innocent to plead guilty to a minor charge to get the whole business over with as quickly as possible and to avoid the chance of a conviction on a more serious charge, and I have known the prosecution accept a plea of guilty to a lesser charge when the accused was clearly guilty of a greater one. Justice does not consist of conviction some people of more, and some of less, than they have done, the average being approximately correct; a man should be exonerated if he has done nothing and convicted of what it is proved that he has done — neither more nor less.

There are two arguments in favour of the system of bargaining in this way, and of extorting swift confessions of guilt.

The first is that it speeds, and therefore increases, justice, for speed (though not precipitousness) is an element of justice. There is obviously something in this argument. No one wants to clog up the courts with last-ditch defences of hopeless cases, at great monetary cost into the bargain. How much worth should be attached to this argument is a matter of judgment, not of ascertainable fact.

The second argument is less compelling. A comparatively swift acknowledgement of guilt is taken as a proxy for remorse, and remorse is supposedly an indicator of a lesser likelihood of repeat offending.

Both the steps in this argument seem to me of doubtful validity. A man's remorse is not to be inferred from a confession from which he derives obvious benefit. There is in any case no way of proving the sincerity of a man's remorse and the connection between even sincere remorse and reoffending is by no means straightforward. Every time I lose my temper I regret it sincerely, but I should not like to claim that as a consequence I shall never lose my temper again, even if my remorse somewhat lengthens the intervals between doing so. Remorse for a crime is not the same as a guarantee that a prisoner will not commit a similar crime. In any case, a man is to be punished for what he has done, not for what he might do in the future.

I changed my opinion on this matter gradually as I worked in the prison, until I was opposed (in theory and, to the extent to which I could be, in practice) to the system of parole, which is intrinsically arbitrary and unjust.

I committed a great error early in my prison career. A prisoner on remand for a serious act of violence took to drawing in his cell. As is often the case with such prisoners when they take to art his drawings were chilling, disturbing and horrific in subject matter. Several times he drew an isolated human eyeball with a dagger driven through it. As he had seriously injured someone in the eye, I sent a copy of the drawing to the judge in the case to suggest how dangerous the prisoner was. This might seem, on first impression, to have been a reasonable thing to do, but in fact it was not — and it was unjust as well as in error.

In the first place, I could not have pointed to any real evidence (other than of the kind that 'it stands to reason' — though what stands to reason often does not happen) that the drawing of violent images was indubitably connected to violent conduct. Even if there had been such evidence, it would have been only statistical in nature.

Let us suppose that, say, eighty per cent of prisoners who drew pictures such as this prisoner's — and what would count as a similar picture would itself be a problem — committed another violent criminal act within a year of leaving prison. What could a judge do, at least justly, with this information if he had it? My sending him the picture drawn by the prisoner was an implicit plea that he give him a longer sentence than he would otherwise have done (or else why send it?), on the grounds of his greater dangerousness.

But in effect it would have been a request to incarcerate the man not for what had been proved beyond reasonable doubt, but for what had an eighty per cent chance of occurring at some time in the future (and a twenty per cent chance of not occurring). Why not, then, imprison someone who has not yet done anything at all, but who can be shown to have an eighty per cent likelihood of committing a violent crime in the future?

Among my duties was the preparation of reports on prisoners for the parole board. I was expected to speculate on the future dangerousness of a prisoner eligible for parole, and this I refused to do before long. I thought it unethical to do so because, even if my speculations were more accurate than could be expected by chance, or more accurate than anyone else's, it was a charade. A man deemed by me to be harmless, or relatively harmless, would be released sooner than a man deemed by me to be dangerous; and this amounted to punishment for crimes a man had not yet committed.

No prisoner was released on parole who had not acknowledged his crime. I suppose most people might think this intuitively to be reasonable. But what of people who stubbornly maintained their innocence after their conviction, some of whom at least, given the fallible nature of human institutions, were right to do so because they were genuinely innocent and wrongly convicted?

I noticed that a number of murderers who had denied for many years the crimes of which they were convicted confessed as the time at which they might be granted parole approached. They might indeed be finally acknowledging what they had done. On the other hand, they might be making a false confession merely to gain release from prison the sooner. If they did not make such a confession, they might spend many more years in prison, as many in fact as they had already spent.

The parole system placed the genuinely innocent man in a horrible dilemma, for a confession once made by someone already convicted would be difficult or impossible to retract, at least with any hope of being believed. On the other hand, the innocence of a man who maintained it despite the obvious advantages of acknowledging guilt could not be presumed therefore to be innocent (though I suspected that a fair proportion of them were). After many years in prison a prisoner might be so institutionalised that he almost feared to be released; and it might also be more important to him to maintain the fiction of his innocence, both for his own sake and that of his family.

In addition to acknowledgment of guilt, remorse was looked for and rewarded by the system of parole.

But since a man's feelings of remorse cannot be directly observed, only expression of remorse could be rewarded — and such expressions are cheap. Of course, anyone listening to or observing expressions of remorse might form an opinion of their sincerity or otherwise, and how far the outer form corresponded to the inner reality. But which of us has never been to the theatre and failed to be convinced by representations of the whole gamut of human emotions?

Parole, then rewards not a laudable or desirable inner state but, at least potentially, acting ability (and punishes its absence). Again, even if our ability to distinguish between fake remorse and true were much better than chance — assuming for a moment what is not true, that remorse can be divided in binary fashion between true and false, with nothing in between — few of us would claim that our ability approached a standard of being beyond reasonable doubt.

In other words, the granting of parole to some and the denial of it to others on grounds that are intrinsically very unsure amounts to arbitrary punishment that it is one of the purposes of law to eliminate. Thus punishment should always be determinate, including for very bad men.

Parole is a manifestation of logocracy, the rule of words, and those who either live by them or are able to manipulate them. But words, as Hobbes said, are wise men's counters while being the money of fools. They are the money of frauds as well, of administrators, careerists and dictators. We have forgotten, if we ever remembered, the words of Kent to Lear when he warns the old man against taking words at face value:

Nor are those empty-hearted whose low sound
Reverbs no hollowness.

6

Suicides

Disease as Commodity

I was about to write 'The worst suicide in prison that I knew…' when I realised how callous the phrase would sound. I would be like one of those unfortunate police spokesmen or spokeswomen (or, these days, spokespersons) deputed to announce the murder of a youth, say to the press, radio and television, who say such things as, 'This was a particularly unnecessary [or pointless or senseless] murder,' as if there were necessary murders. (W.H. Auden, in his suppressed poem about the Spanish Civil War, did speak of 'the necessary murder' — in a positive sense.) It is true, of course, that murders, even those committed on impulse, usually make a certain sense in that they are explicable by the motives of those who commit them. But the sensible murder seems to me like a class without a member, like that of an insect with feathers. If a murder were sensible, it wouldn't be murder — which is not the same as saying it is necessarily committed in a state of madness.

It is customary now for the police spokesman to say that their, the police's, thoughts are with the family of what F.

Tennyson Jesse, the descendent of Alfred Tennyson and writer on murder, called the murderee. Not only is it untrue, it ought to be untrue.

It is untrue because, as anyone who has been around policemen knows, such saccharine compassionate-sounding words do not spring naturally to their lips and correspond to no feeling behind them. The usual mode of speech of policemen, for obvious reasons, is ironical or even cynical. Once, for example, I was in a magistrates' court where a defendant had just been given a fine for some petty offence. He felt this to be an injustice, however, and would not leave the dock, where he stayed protesting vigorously. There were two plain-clothes policemen behind me in the public gallery (you could tell they were policemen by their boot-like shoes, highly-polished) and one said to the other in a lugubrious deadpan about the man in the dock, 'I think 'e needs some 'elp.' The police ought to behave with tact, of course, but the job of the police is not to empathise with the relations of the victim but to bring the culprit to justice — which in my experience is the best therapy possible.

I suppose what I would have meant, had I written, 'the worst suicide in the prison,' was the suicide that caused the most upset to those who witnessed it. The prisoner was a very nasty man who had spent most of his adult life in and out of prison because of his violence to others, and who took stimulant drugs whenever he was able to do so. He had been under the direct and continuous observation of prison officers for some days because of a return to an old habit of his, burning himself on the forearms with lighted cigarettes. His forearms were scarred as if by some smallpox-like disease

— there were now fresh scars at different stages of evolution.

In the day of his suicide, he asked to attend a service in the prison chapel. He had not been known previously to be religious, but the fact is that religious conversion is often a prelude to a decline in criminality, or to 'going straight', as the prisoners put it.

This is not quite the same as saying that religious conversion is the agent of change, for there comes a time when most prisoners want to give up their life of crime. 'I can't do bird no more', they would say. But having reached this point, they need a reason or pretext other than personal defeat for their change of heart, and religious conversion provides a better one than most. My friend and mentor in prison medicine took a rather more cynical view of religious conversion in prison among long-term prisoners. When asked one day by the Parole Board why it was that so many of the prisoners seem to have converted, he replied 'I expect it's because they want a change of diet' — many of the religions or cults to which they converted having various dietary restrictions. It always pleased prisoners to make difficulties or complications for the authorities.

On the subject of religion, I detected no great religious enthusiasm among Moslems, mainly of Pakistani descent. This was, however, more than ten years ago. Things may have changed since. They did not pray, they did not keep Ramadan (except as a delaying tactic when they were called to court), they did not demand halal food, and as far as I could tell, they paid no particular attention to their imam, a pleasant, mild-mannered, timid and almost obsequious man. In fact, they were on the whole hard-line strays whose main religious preoccupation (in fact, more social than religious) was to preserve the system of arranged and forced marriages — arranged for the men and forced for the women.

There was one small group of Moslems, however, who were more observant, those of Jamaican descent, now called Afro-Caribbean despite the fact that they are of the second generation born in this country (perhaps they should be called Afro-Saxon). It was amusing to see their girlfriends arrive at the prison to visit them with their young off-spring, who shortly before had worn the scantiest of clothing, but were now draped in crow-black clothes, covering everything except their eyes. Since it is likely that their grandparents, in particular their grand-mothers, were pious evangelical or Pentecostal Christians who went to church impeccably dressed in gloves and hat every Sunday, there to speak in tongues, it is worth wondering what the attraction of Islam was for these prisoners.

I think we may safely exclude what Gibbon, in another context of religious conversion, calls 'the truth of the doctrine itself', as theirs was not a group of people much concerned with arcane or abstruse questions of truth in general. Having usually been sexually promiscuous and predatory in their recent past, like most of their compeers, Islam gave them a means of controlling their women better, for while promiscuous and predatory, they always neverthe-less wanted the exclusive sexual possession of someone as a prop to their ego. Religion was a way of making this easier.

A second attraction of Islam was that, while wanting a pretext to give up their life of crime, they wanted also to feel that they had not altogether surrendered to the society around them, for that would signal their defeat. How better, then, to abandon crime but oppose society than to take up Islam, which they knew to be feared and disliked by most white society? Islam for them killed two birds with one stone. It gave them a reason to give up common crime, but allowed them to maintain their oppositional and defiant attitude to society. I did occasionally find a Koran, or other Islamic literature, obviously directed at converts and conversion, in drawers throughout the prison (but never a Bible or Christian literature).

In my time, not a single graduate of the prison was ever convicted of a terrorist act or conspiracy, but a young man did once confide in me that his ambition was to be a suicide-bomber. His mother was British and his father Arab. In a different era, he would have wanted to pass as British, but times change and it is deemed more heroic now to be a member of a minority, and he called himself an Arab.

The young man was very unpleasant and had a long history of criminal violence (as well as of taking drugs). Violence was his only method of obtaining what he wanted. Although not tall, he was built like an armoured vehicle, and seemed to be armour-plated against pain. He was ugly, but not only in a physical sense — an ugliness of soul manifested itself in his expressions. He was imprisoned this time for violence towards his wife, which he regarded as his right. Sometimes, when he was frustrated, he would charge out of his cell at full speed and into the wall opposite, using his head as a battering ram. He bore the pain of it well and said he was in training for things to come.

One day he told me that, on his release from prison, he

would kill himself by blowing himself up in a public place, taking as many people with him as he could. Should I — was I obliged to — tell the police? I called my medical defence agency and spoke to one of their lawyers. If I thought that the man had meant what he said, he told me, I should tell the police; but at the same time I should tell my patient that I was doing so.

This struck me as among the most idiotic advice that I have ever received on any subject. In the first place, the man of necessity remained my patient; in the second, to make an open enemy of him was hazardous for me; and in the third, it would hamper the work of the secret service.

As it happened, I had a friend who worked for the secret service and I asked him to put me in touch with it. He gave me the number of someone to call, and I told him about the prisoner. He thanked me for the information and a couple of weeks later called to thank me again and to tell me that the man had already been known to them and would be subject to close surveillance when he left prison. I have never heard of him since.

The question of the false positive — a man assumed wrongly to be at high risk of dangerous behaviour — always haunted me. I had a patient, a young man, who donned military costume, though he had never been a soldier, a fashion of dressing that I always find somewhat sinister. In addition, he had sewn a little Federal German flag on his arm, which one could not help but suppose was an acceptable symbol of support for a previously unacceptable regime.

There were several things about this young man that worried me. He was socially isolated, except for having joined a gun-club; he mainly sat at home reading war books. In addition, though, he was a militant vegetarian and lover of animals. He told me that when he went to his local supermarket (where I sometimes shopped) he was so angered by the meat-counter — because of the cruel conditions in which animals raised for meat were kept — that he felt as if he could gun down all the people standing at it. He said it through the gritted teeth of someone who could barely control his anger.

I was worried that he might one day act on his plan, desire or fantasy, that one day he would indeed gun down people in the supermarket. Then it would be found that he had been my patient and I had done nothing to prevent him from killing in this way. I would be deemed more responsible for the deaths of the victims than he — I would be vilified. Since his threat was so vague and non-specific, however, I told no one (except his own doctor) and of course to this day, more than a quarter of a century later, I have not heard of any massacre by him. He is now past the massacring age; but for a number of years I should not have been surprised to have heard that he had committed a mass-killing.

To return, after this long digression, to 'the worst suicide I have known', the man was taken, as he asked, to the prison chapel. There were reasons other than religious sentiment why prisoners asked to go to the chapel. It was a break in routine and was said to be a location for dealing and plotting. But since religion was officially approved of, and moreover its exercise was regarded as a human right, any prisoner who wanted to could not very well be denied access, except if he was raving mad.

The prisoner was accompanied by two officers but he was not handcuffed. Suddenly, as he walked through the central tower of the Victorian part of the prison, he broke away from the officers and did what no one had ever done before or had believed possible. He clambered up the smooth and slippery tiled wall to a considerable height — like the count scaling the walls of Castle Dracula — and then plunged headfirst on to the stone floor below. He was killed instantly. Needless to say, the two officers who had accompanied him were deeply shaken.

It is a matter of conjecture how soon their thoughts turned to fear of the blame that might be attached to them for this unforeseen event. It is a principal of modern management (not only in prison) that there is always someone to blame. And that person shall be the lowest in the hierarchy who can plausibly be the object. A metal grille was soon installed in the tower to prevent a repetition.

Prisoners did not seem to regard the suicide of one of their number as very tragic. Indeed, in so far as a suicide was an embarrassment to the prison authorities, the prisoners welcomed and even connived at it. Once, for example, we had a prisoner who was a notorious slasher of himself with knives or razors, whose resultant injuries were life-threatening rather than merely mildly disfiguring — usually the case with most prisoners who cut themselves. He had several times nearly bled to death, and was so difficult to handle that he was sent from prison to prison. He caused so much anxiety that each prison took its turn in overseeing him.

He was under the direct observation of two prison officers

when he nonetheless managed to cut his throat badly enough to need an operation outside prison. He had insinuated a razor blade between his gum and his inner cheek and at a moment when the officers' vigilance was distracted for a moment, he took it out and slashed his throat.

How had he obtained the razor? Someone in the kitchen, or in charge of the food on its way from the kitchen to his cell, had slipped it into the mashed potato serve to him. He could not use it immediately, but bided his time.

He did not die; the operation on his throat was a success. He was not really suicidal and was proud of his success, like a veteran of a war, or rather wars. He was the Coriolanus of self-mutilation. He was also a recidivist armed-robber. No one understood him, least of all me. What would the understanding be, what would be the *Eureka* moment at which one could say, '*Now* I understand him'?

This being a prison, one apparent suicide turned out to be a murder. I was on duty overnight when the phone rang at three in the morning.

'Can you come to the prison, Sir? There's been a death in custody.'

'A death in custody' was the phrased used, as if deaths in custody were a phenomenon apart, completely different from all other deaths. In a sense they were. With the state *in loco parentis*, as it were, to all those detained at its behest, it assumed a greater degree of responsibility for them than for more civic-minded citizens.

The prisoner was certainly dead when I arrived in the prison. He had, in fact, been dead for some time. He was lying on his bed on which the officers had placed him after trying to resuscitate him on the ground. It had all been quite hopeless. He had been stone dead when they cut him down from the noose by which he had apparently hanged himself (officers all carry special scissors for this purpose).

I examined him, nonetheless, and certified him dead. Then I spoke to his cellmate who had been in the cell with him when he hanged himself. He claimed to have woken in his sleep, seen the man hanging and pressed the emergency bell straight away. But I thought he was strangely unmoved by the experience, being utterly, even icily, calm and detached about it. I recorded this in the notes. On an admittedly small, number of occasions when I had a similar task to perform, the prisoner involved had always been shaken, usually trembling quite severely. This man was quite without emotion.

Another very strange thing was that he refused the sleeping tablet I offered him. Only on very rare occasions did I prescribe such a tablet. As such tablets were currency in the prison, to prescribe them soon turned into a rod with which the prisoners beat the doctor's back — the prisoner for whom they were prescribed would soon return and demand more, growing angry if refused. It was almost unheard-of for a prisoner to turn down the offer of a sleeping tablet, but this man did so, evidently confident of getting back to sleep as if nothing had happened. I also recorded his most unusual refusal in the notes.

On my way out of the prison, a prisoner in a cell nearby to his called me over to him. The news of the hanging had already spread.

He told me that he had been a friend of the hanged man and that he had walked with him in the exercise yard only that afternoon, when he had appeared not the least depressed and had been looking forward to his imminent release from prison. This, too, I recorded in the notes, and I was later glad that I did. I thanked the friend of the deceased for his information.

What, though, had he meant by it? This appeared to be no ordinary suicide, in so far as any suicide is ordinary. It became clear the next day — or rather, later the same day.

A prisoner approached me and said, 'Excuse me, doctor, can I have a word with you?' When a prisoner asked that, I never refused; it was always something important. I took him to my room.

'I'm not a grass, doctor,' he said. 'You know that, don't you? I'm not a grass. [A grass in an informer and to grass is to inform. He 'grassed me up' is to be informed upon by someone.] You won't grass me up, will you, doctor?' He feared I might tell other prisoners my source of information: grass on a grass.

'No, of course not.'

'I'm not a grass, doctor, I'm definitely not a grass, I don't want you to think that I am, but I think I ought to tell you something.'

What he had to tell me was that he had been put in the same cell as the man who had shared the cell with the apparent suicide, and that he had boasted that he had hanged the dead man.

He had given the victim a choice: to have his throat cut while he slept or to fake a suicide by hanging himself. Evidently the deceased, terrified of his cellmate and afraid to call the officers, could think of no way out of the choice but to hang himself. The culprit made the noose from the victim's bedding and pushed away the chair from under him.

I thanked my informant and told him that I had to call the police, giving them his name. I reassured him that the other prisoners would not consider him a grass because they — mostly — drew the line at murder, especially as cowardly and one-sided a murder as this (a fair fight would have been different). But if he were still afraid, he could be protected. I called the police, gave a statement and heard no more about it until I was called to court to give my evidence.

The accused had by then confessed to the police and had corroborated his story by telling them that he had flushed the razor with which he had threatened the deceased down the cell lavatory, where they then found it. The accused was a violent criminal who had spent much of his life in prison and the records going back many years had to be searched for unexpected deaths of cell-mates throughout his prison career.

There was none, but powerful testimony was given at his trial. Another prisoner who had shared a cell with him described how he had discussed with the accused how best to get admission to the hospital wing, where the prison regime was more relaxed and comfortable. The accused had told him of a wangle that would certainly work. The witness would pretend to hang himself and the accused would call an officer. The witness was certain to be admitted to the hospital wing thereafter.

The plan went well — at first. But when the witness was choking on his noose, the accused did not call the officer, instead looking at the witness and laughing. Luckily an officer happened to look through the judas-window in the door and rushed in to save the witness; the accused pretended just to have woken and to have been about to call the officers. The witness had not dared to reveal the truth to the officers, and the accused was believed.

On another occasion, I was walking through the prison when there was what was called 'a whistle alarm'. Even in these hi-tech days there was no better way of signalling an emergency than the prison officer's whistle, the sound of which carried through the prison and always indicated the direction from which it came. I carried such a whistle but never had to use it and doubt that I would have had the presence of mind to do so if I had. And to use it when it was unnecessary was the prison equivalent of pulling the emergency cord to stop a train.

A whistle alarm was always followed by the sound of officers rushing to the scene. When it was in the Victorian part of the prison it was an impressive sound: it was disciplined, there was no shouting, only the echoing sound of scores of men running along the ironwork passageways, both urgent and matter-of-fact. Other officers locked the prisoners back in their cells to prevent them from taking advantage of the situation.

On this occasion, it was a prisoner who had hanged himself. I had a message to go at once to his cell. He was on the ground unconscious, having been cut down. His heart had stopped and he was not breathing. We managed to resuscitate him; he had not been hanging for long and it seemed as if he had almost arranged to be found before he died, though it was a very fine calculation and a near miss. A cry for help, a sign of distress?

My wife's favourite prison story was of the time I was called to the prison in the early hours one morning when a prison officer was called to a cell by the bell pressed by a prisoner who was making a noose for himself. When I arrived in the prison, the officer was sitting next to the prisoner. It was a very very early hour of the morning.

'The things you 'ave to do for 'umanity, sir,' he said as I arrived all bleary-eyed.

'You what?' said the prisoner.

''umanity,' said the officer, and turned to him. 'You're 'uman, aren't you?'

Even slight gestures had to be taken seriously, however. It is one of the enduring myths, which somehow seems ineradicable by mere evidence and argument, that people who talk about or make gestures in the direction of suicide never actually commit suicide. Perhaps this myth is the result of a false syllogism: if most people who talk of suicide or make suicidal gestures never commit suicide, then people who commit suicide never talk about it or make suicidal gestures. But none of this means either, of course, that suicidal gestures aren't used as emotional blackmail to bring others to heel.

The young man who had hanged himself came — or was brought — round. We were very pleased with ourselves for having saved a life and were rather disappointed that the young man did not seem to appreciate how close to death he had been. Nor was he particularly grateful. Girlfriend trouble had prompted his suicide action. A few months later we received notification that he was suing the prison for not having prevented him from hanging himself in the first place.

The case was settled out of court, probably for a few thousand, it being more expensive to defend the case than to settle it this way. The prisoner had taken a leaf from Falstaff's book: 'I will turn diseases to commodity.'

7

Dr No

Manacles of the Mind

Gratitude was rare among prisoners, for obvious reasons, and like many rare things it was precious, at least to me. They generally took for granted that they could see a doctor almost any time they liked (or could in those days; the system has changed, and not for the better) as most people take running water for granted, as if it had always existed. An editorial in the *British Medical Journal* suggested that prisoners should have the right to the same medical care as everyone else, whereupon our Senior Medical Officer wrote a letter to point out that this would be an excellent and very beneficial idea — for everyone who was not a prisoner. Where else in the country, he asked, could you see a doctor within two hours of requesting to do so?

Prisoners were, on average, operated on sooner for their 'cold,' or non-emergency, conditions than if they had been 'on the out,' when they would be stuck on a waiting list. A man at a party asked me about getting his hernia repaired as quickly as possible on the NHS. 'Commit an imprisonable offence,' I said. I would send a prisoner to a surgeon and he would operate within a week or two.

Every now and then prison officers would ask me to see a prisoner who was not, in their opinion, 'your typical con.' This was a compliment to the man referred to. One day they brought me a man on remand who was not 'your typical con.' Even a man on remand, yet to be tried and officially and legally still an innocent man, is still a 'con' (short for convict) to the officers, for whom there is no smoke without fire.

He was a first-timer and a few years older than most first-timers. Although we are constantly, and no doubt correctly, told that there is no such thing as the criminal type, this man would certainly not have been of that type if it existed. He was soft-spoken, mild-mannered and a respectable member of the skilled working class who had never been unemployed and who had always provided for his two daughters, to whom he had given old-fashioned names suggesting great tenderness towards them. I took this as an indication of his decency.

The question of names is an interesting one. There was certainly an excess of young men in prison with non-traditional names such as Lee or Dwayne. Indeed, there were so many of the former that I once mooted that all Lees should be arrested at birth and kept in preventive detention. The literal minded would say that preventive detention is very bad on principle, as if I had meant to be taken literally. They might point out that not all Lees by any means are criminals — though they would also deny that the categories of criminal and non-criminal exist, everyone being criminal. By such arguments generalisations become impossible, at least on certain subjects, and people are able to screen out disturbing or unpleasant realities from their minds. Knowing precisely what realities must be screened out of the mind is a large part of maintaining a modern reputation for decency.

I took the remand prisoner's history. He had been married for more than ten years when, three of four months ago his wife had left him suddenly for another man. He was devastated by this; he said that as far as he was aware, he had done nothing to drive her away (except, possibly, boring her). While it is always necessary in such cases to hear both sides, if not more, of the story, I believed him, partly because I wanted to. My guess was that, having married young, his wife had missed the wildness of youth, and now sought belatedly to make up for it: for it is possible to settle down too early as well as too late.

Be that as it may, he was left with two children whom the mother had deserted, a demanding full-time job, and a deep emotional upset. He began to do what he had never done before: drink too much. As a result, he could not sleep properly. He went to his doctor to complain of his insomnia, and his doctor prescribed a sleeping tablet for him. On the first night on which he took it, he went to the pub where he normally drank and set about destroying it.

He did not remember what he had done, nor could he give any reason for it. He certainly gained nothing by it. He had no animus against the pub, where he had always behaved impeccably. He got on well with the landlord and had no motive of revenge. Before he took the sleeping tablet, he had drunk five pints of beer.

I sent for the general practitioner's notes to corroborate the story. It was in the days when doctors sent the notes without charge for the good of the patient. Now they are a matter of commerce, though electronic transfer has made the sharing of information almost costless.

The notes confirmed the prisoner's story.

I wrote a report to his lawyer in which I said that the sleeping pill he had been prescribed had the rare side-effect of paradoxical excitation, often with insensate violence, especially when the patient had drunk alcohol. Here was a perfect, one might say textbook, case of the side-effect. I sent copies of the scientific literature with my report so that no one should think I was merely advocating on a patient with whom I sympathised, but was presenting an objective case. I hoped that my report, of which I was secretly rather proud, would lead to his immediate release at his trial.

A little while after his trial I was walking through the prison when he approached me.

'I wanted to thank you for what you did for me, doctor,' he said.

'I didn't do anything for you,' I replied, not quite sincerely.

'Your report helped me a lot. The judge said that without it he would have given me twice the sentence.'

I told him that I was disappointed that he had not been released immediately. The judge had said, however, that the attack on the pub was so serious, the damage so great, and the episode so frightening to the other customers, that he had to impose a prison sentence: but more than this, because the box in which the sleeping tablets had been given him had a warning on the label to the effect that the pills should not be taken with drink. In disregarding this warning, the prisoner had made himself responsible for the consequences.

I am a hard-liner on crime and believe the courts are generally too lenient — sometimes absurdly so — but I thought that in this case the judge was too harsh.

It relieved me to think this, because it reassured me that my views on crime were not motivated by sadism. It is true that the label told him not to drink and take the pills. But surely he, or any sensible person, must have thought that the warning was for his own safety rather that for that of the public, as indeed it mainly was. Not one person in a thousand would have anticipated such a reaction to the drug and I do not think the prisoner could have reasonably foreseen it. Failing to heed the warnings on a packet or bottle of pills may be foolish but it is hardly criminal. I understand that those who witnessed his violent outburst might have been dissatisfied if the judge had dealt with him leniently; but justice is justice, not pleasing the crowd. I have known many a man walk free from court with only a fraction of the excuse this man had for what he did.

He thanked me again for my report and my efforts on his behalf. As I parted from him I was moved not only by his gratitude but even more by his calm and unembittered acceptance of his fate, his equanimity in the face of the law's severity. I thought he was a good man and I have always hoped that this episode in his life had no lingering effect upon the rest of it — or on the life of his daughters.

About the same time there was another case in which a prescription played an important part. In this case the man was considerably older, with two grown daughters. He was an alcoholic who had separated from his wife and he freely admitted that it was his own drinking, and consequent financial irresponsibility, that had driven his wife away. He could not blame her, he said; he made no excuses for himself. He was another untypical 'con'.

His crime was also a strange and unusual one. He had gone to the doctor complaining of depression (no one uses the word unhappiness these days, all deviation from a state of permanent bliss being considered an illness), and his doctor had prescribed him antidepressants, as doctors almost always do these days in these circumstances. At the time of the consultation, the patient ascribed his drinking to his depression rather than the other way round, which is much more common (though some people do drink to excess because of a depressed mood and not otherwise).

He took the pills as directed but did not stop drinking. One days shortly after he started taking the pills, having had a drink but not yet drunk, he was walking down a residential street when he heard the voice of his wife calling out for help coming from a house. She shouted (so he thought) that she was being attacked and was in need of rescue. He took her voice to be real, rushed up to the house, and knocked furiously at the door. Receiving no immediate answer, he broke a front window with a punch, with the true madman's disregard of his own safety, and climbed in and found the startled householder, an elderly man, with the screams of his wife for help still ringing in his ears. He demanded to know of the old man the whereabouts of his wife, and what he was doing to her. The elderly man, bewildered by these events, gave no answer apart from, 'What are you talking about?', and demanded that the interloper should leave his house: whereupon the hallucinated man attacked him and beat him severely in an attempt to extract the information from him.

(No one really believes that torture does not work.) Fortunately neighbours and passers-by heard the commotion and intervened before the elderly man was seriously injured or killed.

This conduct was completely uncharacteristic of the accused, who admittedly was a drunk — but a quiet drunk, whose worst excesses when inebriated were the passing of silly remarks and the failure to meet his obligations. The latter was chronic, tiring the patience of his family, employers and friends. He had never been arrested before, however, not even for the most minor offence. Moreover, he was in his fifties, which is a most unusual age at which to commence criminal.

Examining his records, I was able to write a report on his behalf to the effect that his extraordinary behaviour was provoked by his medication. It was known sometimes to cause, often when taken with alcohol, vivid hallucinations, as it had done in this case. People with hallucinations may in time come to recognise them as such, but when they start suddenly they are initially taken by the sufferer to be true perceptions, and often act on them as if they were, as had this man. A colleague in the hospital next door, who was much more distinguished in the profession than I, wrote a report confirming mine.

The result was exactly the same as in the previous case — a sentence half as long as the accused would otherwise have received.

But in this case, no doubt somewhat inconsistently, I thought the sentence correct. In part no doubt because a prolonged separation from alcohol was very necessary for him and would do him good, as turned out to be the case.

And this was despite my general opposition to the idea of prison as a therapeutic institution, a hospital for the illness of criminality.

I got to know the man well and came not only to like but to respect him. He was highly intelligent, a man who, if he had not had such a liking for alcohol, would have had a successful career despite humble beginnings. Apart from his weakness — admittedly an important one — he was a man of good character. He later recognised that going to prison had a positive effect on his life, though he had found it deeply unpleasant, because it allowed him time to reflect upon his own biography, something he had previously avoided. It is only by thinking biographically that one can come to realise one's own contribution to one's misfortunes and thereby (possibly) avoid making the same mistakes in the future, and resist the sour, entrapping satisfactions of resentment. Few of us manage it wholly, and it is impressive when one sees it in others.

He was born into the working class, in the days when there was still regular industrial work for it to do. Conditions in his childhood were hard, though, unimaginably so for people born in a later age. There were, for example, no indoor lavatories. Several houses shared the same outdoor latrine — never luxurious and a torture in winter. At the same time there was a social solidarity that gave a warmth to human existence. It was unnecessary to lock front doors for no one stole from anyone else, and not merely from lack of anything to steal. There is always something to steal, and in poverty the marginal value of everything increases.

Though he had left school as was then customary at the

age of fourteen — customary because staying at school was neither financially feasible for his parents nor seen by them as a route out of poverty — he had nevertheless received, or acquired by his own efforts, a far better basic education than is common in his class today. He wrote and spoke grammatically; his vocabulary was extensive; his powers of logic were highly developed, as his subsequent career demonstrated; he was a keen observer of the world around him and he read widely and intelligently. He was ordinary neither in his tastes nor his manner; he was a civilised human being notwithstanding his serious weakness. He reminded me of something that I had learnt in Africa, that poverty is not the same as degradation.

I spent many hours talking to him — as long as I was able to — and one thing he said etched itself on my mind. We were talking about art for some reason — I can't remember what — and I asked him whether he had ever been to the National Gallery. No, he replied, and I asked him why not.

'We thought it wasn't for people like us', he said.

Not for people like us: how deeply revealing these words were. Here was a man who by temperament and intelligence would have gained more sustenance from the gallery than many a person who enters it from a sense of duty, but who was kept out of it by some magnetic force, in his own mind, of repulsion. To change the metaphor, Blake's 'the mind-forg'd manacles' struck me as expressing forcefully an important phenomenon of which this is an instance. We make difficulties for ourselves when there are none; and stone walls do not a prison make.

I continued to see him as an out-patient in the hospital

next door once he had left prison. I had no scientific evidence that to do so would do him any good, and I had no medical means of preventing him from drinking. But I thought intuitively that the mere expression of interest in his life might encourage him. Whether or not I played any part in his sobriety, he did not drink for at least the three years in which I continued to see him, a period of abstinence longer than any other in his adult life.

He always said that his period in prison had been extremely salutary and beneficial to him. He did not believe that he would have stopped drinking without it. During one of our chats — I could not call them anything else, though they became less frequent as the period of his abstinence lengthened — I asked him what the prisoners thought of me.

'Hard but fair,' he said.

This was a glass half-full and half-empty. Of course I was pleased to be known as fair or just. I wanted to be known and respected as a person who could, and did, distinguish between true and false distress, and who would do whatever he could, medically and otherwise, to help prisoners, and even to protect them from injustice.

But to be thought hard rather than firm did not please me. I tried to convince myself that my interlocutor had meant firm rather than hard, that he had chosen the wrong word as we all sometimes do, and that he meant the softer term. But he was the second ex-prisoner I had met who had used the word, and that could scarcely be a coincidence.

I am not an uncritical believer in the theory of the invariably deep significance of the first thing that comes into your head, but on this occasion I thought there was something to it. The first word was the one that counted. I resolved thereafter on a slightly less forthright approach, though without compromising on my general principle that I should not prescribe medication in prison unless it were strictly indicated. If this principle, *per impossibile*, were observed outside prison, the pharmaceutical industry would be bankrupt within the week.

I quickly learned in prison that to be loved by the prisoners was not a desirable or even a possible goal. Their so-called love would have been of the mere cupboard variety, that is to say love for what they thought they could have got out of me. I was not like the Prince for whom it was wiser to be feared than loved, but I wanted, or thought it important, to be respected rather than loved — in the very strange circumstances of prison. I wanted to be known as someone over whose eyes the wool could not easily be pulled but who, at the same time, would relieve genuine suffering and not miss a diagnosis.

This was a narrow path to tread, and I would not claim that I never strayed from it in either direction, for as Hippocrates said some time ago, judgment is difficult. But it must be exercised or the results will be worse overall. When, towards the very end of my career in prison, new and inexperienced doctors were brought in to perform most of the medical work, it was not long before a third of the prisoners were prescribed opioid analgesics for which in practically no case was there medical indication.

This incontinent prescribing was the consequence of the belief that all protestations of suffering are equal, and therefore equally to be sympathised with. To be sympathetic requires that the patients' word must be taken literally and at face value, including the demand for medication to relieve the suffering expressed. Irrespective of the moral validity of this argument, it did not pacify the prisoners but inflamed them rather. The doses were never high enough ('It's not 'olding me, doctor,' they would say, 'it's just not 'olding me'), whereas an initial refusal would prevent escalation from the outset.

I was later told that I was known in the prison as Dr No, that is to say as someone who refused to prescribe on request. Of course, that is not the same as saying that I never prescribed. While I always explained my reasons for refusal, some did not want to listen to them.

'I thought you was 'ere to 'elp me,' they would say.

'I'm here to do what I think is right for you.'

This was unfashionably paternalistic. There are many for whom what they want and what is right or good for them is a distinction without a difference. But it seems to me that a doctor cannot, and ought not, to avoid paternalism altogether.

I remember, for example, a middle-aged prisoner who had moderately-raised blood pressure. I explained to him the increase risk of stroke or heart attack that he ran, and the reduction of the risk if he took medication for the rest of his life. I explained to him how many people in his situation needed to take the medication in order that one person should avoid a single heart attack or stroke, adding that unfortunately for the moment it was impossible to predict which of the patients taking the medication would be the lucky one. Finally I told him some of the possible, but not likely, side-effects of the medication that I proposed.

Having been given all this information, necessary for

informed consent — though there is always more information — I asked him whether he wanted to take the treatment.

'I don't know,' he said. 'You're the doctor.'

This seemed to me a perfectly reasonable reply. What was the point of going to the doctor if you have to decide everything for yourself? You consult a doctor for his advice, not merely for the information on which to base a decision. A few times in my life I have resigned myself into the care of doctors and I have not had cause to regret it.

Though he was neither an educated nor an intelligent man, the prisoner posed a pertinent second question:

'Would you take it if you was me, doctor?'

The answer was what Donald Rumsfeld would no doubt have called 'unstraightforwardly straightforward'. There were at least two questions here: what would I do if I were a rational man, and what would I in practice do?

The problem with the first question is that there is no way of answering it even in principle. One man might think it worthwhile to run the increased statistical risk for the convenience of not taking tablets every day, while another might think the inconvenience well worth it. I do not see how the risk and inconvenience can be reduced to a single scale of measurement such that it would allow of a purely rational way of deciding between the two courses of action.

The second question, what I should do in practice, was fortunately more easily answered. Like the majority of mankind I would not take the medication as prescribed even if I intended to do so. Man loves to take medicine, but not as prescribed and not every day. At least a half of people prescribed medication to lower blood pressure have given up within a year and the other half take it intermittently, only when they remember. The prisoner seemed to me to be in that small category of persons who take their medication assiduously, precisely as prescribed.

'If I were you,' I said, 'I wouldn't take it.'

And just to make sure that he did not feel the slightest twinge of anxiety or guilt about not taking it, emotions that would only poison his existence, I added that I was sure that he was not going to have a stroke or heart attack, though of course I could be sure of no such thing.

Sometimes there are matters more important than truth.

8

Encouraging Thwacks

'You are British, not Albanian.'

My alcoholic patient was, as I have said, a highly-intelligent man; and being adept at computers he started an internet business immediately on his release. He spotted a niche that had not been filled and within a three weeks had made more money than I earned in six months.

I found this enterprise both astonishing and reassuring: astonishing because it was so alien to me and reassuring because it meant that, for all the obstacles placed in people's path (and that they place there themselves) ours is still a partly open society, at least economically. I don't believe that wealth is itself evidence of virtue, but in my patient's case I was very impressed by what I assumed would be his accession to great wealth, the result of applied intelligence after many reverses in life.

I was surprised, therefore, when he told me that he had given up his business just as it was taking off. There was no reason, at the rate it grew, why he should not have been a millionaire within a year. But, he told me, that he knew and mistrusted himself. The moment things began to go well for him was the moment he began to go off the rails and think he could drink with impunity. He would indulge then in fantasies of omnipotence, and it was best to stop before they began.

The Duchess of Windsor once put it that you can never be too rich. For most people who have made a deal of money, wealth becomes not something to enjoy but an end in itself, or very nearly so: perhaps an assurance of prowess and of power over others. I had a friend who, having made a reasonable fortune early in his thirties, devoted the rest of his life to philosophy and contemplation in surroundings of beauty. Apart from my patient, he was the only person I have ever known who could have become immensely rich by merely continuing his activity yet spurned the opportunity for the sake of another end.

There was another prisoner whom I admired, though this time in spite of myself.

I asked him to see me because I wanted information about his cell-mate, whom I suspected of having become psychotic. Did he talk to himself, did he express paranoid notions, did he act in an inexplicable way, did he appear to attend to stimuli that only he could perceive?

The prisoner, a man in his fifties (old for prison), entered my room with a volume of Wittgenstein under his arm. Suffice it to say that Wittgenstein is not the favourite reading of prisoners, and I therefore concluded that the man before me had been convicted of fraud, and probably an elaborate one at that. So it turned out.

We fell to talking and he told me that he had not much time left to serve. 'Serving' a prison sentence has always seemed to me an odd locution. To whom or to what is the 'service' rendered? Similarly, prisoners, and others, say at the end of their sentence that they have 'paid their debt to society,' but this seems to me even odder.

After all, it is said that it currently costs about £40,000 a year to keep a prisoner in prison and, therefore, if anything a prisoner's 'debt to society', if that is what it is, has mounted still further by the end of his sentence, and is most unlikely ever to be paid.

Crime is not double-entry book-keeping, with crime on one side and punishment on the other. Imprisonment cannot mean serving, nor paying, a debt. The notorious child-murderer Myra Hindley used to claim, after decades in prison, that she had paid her debt to society as a reason for her release. But could someone spend decades in prison in advance and then claim on release the right to kill children?

The prisoner now before me told me that a fortune awaited him on his release, whose whereabouts he had refused to disclose to the authorities. If he had disclosed the whereabouts his prison sentence would have been shorter, but as a true *homo economicus* he had calculated that, by spending an extra three years in prison, he would in effect 'earn' £12,000,000 a year.

Most of his three extra years had been spent in an open prison where conditions had been far from abominable, even resembling those of a country club, and he had been sent back to closed prison — where we met — for a short time before his release. He also complimented the prison service on its good treatment of him, and he had always found prison, if not agreeable, tolerable — if he had access to the likes of Wittgenstein to read.

His crime was tax fraud — Value Added Tax to be precise. It was a victimless crime, or at least a crime whose victims were so numerous that they would not have noticed their own victimisation — say a pound of tax revenue from each that would have to be raised some other way (and possibly wasted of course). I found it difficult to work up any moral indignation against this as I did when, for example, a patient of mine — an old lady who paid for everything in cash — withdrew a thousand pounds from her building society savings account to pay for an air ticket to a distant ill sister before she died and was robbed of it by two young men who were waiting outside the building society for just a victim such as she.

I even saw him as some kind of hero, though he was no Robin Hood. He robbed the rich not to help the poor but to live in luxury in some tropical paradise. But no one can be so respectable, surely, that he does not rejoice or applaud when the authorities, especially the tax authorities, are made a monkey of by a clever individual — who thinks of the taxman as his friend? The prisoner's fraud was so complex and involved that I could not understand it even when he explained it to me (even my own tax form is beyond my comprehension). The fraud was the product of an ingenious and sophisticated mind that had now turned to Wittgenstein, and we tend to admire in others what we could not do ourselves.

Educated middle-class people often wonder how they would cope with or survive imprisonment. The answer is that they would survive it very well, most of them, often better than the poorer and less-educated. They assume it would be a nightmare for them, and so it would be at first. But strangely enough they adapt and make a life for themselves, at least in conditions that are minimally decent. They are better able than the less intelligent and educated to distance themselves from their own immediate experience, observing it as if it belonged to someone else as it were. Class hostility towards them, if it exists, does not last long, for the prisoners soon find uses for them, such as writing letters, examination of their cases, and so forth. They soon are awarded a certain prestige.

I have been arrested only three times in my life ('I don't call that bad, do you', as the prison officer put it). But each time it was so farcical that I had difficulty in taking it seriously. I was arrested in Honduras and deported as a Marxist revolutionary; I was arrested in Gabon as a South African spy; and I was arrested in Albania as a meddlesome journalist. Only on the last of these occasions was there a semblance of seriousness (seriousness for me, that is), but it did not last very long.

I was deported from Honduras to Nicaragua after I had driven into it from El Salvador in my pick-up truck, a young soldier, who was mostly asleep, pointing his gun into my side as I drove. I had to buy him lunch as he was only a poor recruit, and I felt rather sorry for my captor, who would have to hitch a lift back from the Nicaraguan border afterwards. I was in the custody of a Gabonese policeman who had arrested me as I climbed down from a truck in which I had been given a lift until he realised that I was a doctor, whereupon he asked for advice about his venereal disease in return for my liberation (he had walked around the chair in which I was sitting in the police station, saying admiringly, '*Vous avez beaucoup de papier dans la tête*', you have a lot of paper in your head, the highest praise). Only in Albania did my arrest lead to imprisonment, however brief. It was shortly after the downfall of communism there and a cardiologist, Dr Sali Berish, was now in charge. There was a demonstration in Skanderbeg Square, the very centre of the capital Tirana by old communists, unhappy at their loss of power. The police attacked them with baton charges, driving them before them, and I took photographs of them doing so. Suddenly my arm was gripped from behind by a policeman who hauled me to a nearby paddy-wagon, giving me an encouraging thwack on the back with his baton to help me in. There were two other men, Albanians, already in the wagon, one of whom spoke fluent English.

'So that's democracy!' he said.

We careened at high speed through the streets of Tirana (in those days there was still no traffic — the absence of traffic being one of the undoubted benefits of communist rule — as though our incarceration were a matter of urgency. We arrived at a suburban police station where we were thrown into the same cell, again with a couple of baton blows on the back to encourage us not to dither. (I was subsequently rather proud of my bruises.)

Once in the cell we could hear other prisoners being beaten in cells nearby. We did not know why they were under arrest but assumed that it was all part of normal police practice, for the eradication of such traditions is not the work of a moment. The police were presumably exemplifying one of the laws of dialectical materialism, the unity of opposites:

where once they had beaten anti-communists, now they beat communists. The goals change, the methods remains the same.

My two Albanian co-detainees began to shout and wail. One of them banged on the iron door of the cell. I spoke to the one who had fluent English.

'You must stop this,' I said, 'or you'll get us all beaten. From now on you're British, not Albanian. You will remain silent.'

Strangely enough, my command worked. They stopped, though this had the effect of making the cries of the beaten all the clearer. After about half an hour the cell door opened and I was beckoned out. I was to be released on the orders of the Minister of the Interior, with whose chief adviser I had dined the night before and who was most anxious for the reputation of the new regime. Word of my incarceration had reached him through my friends who had witnessed my arrest.

But should I consent to be released while my two co-detainees were still detained? I had to decide in a split-second whether to play the hero and refuse. I had pointed out when first arrested that I had a plane to catch that very day which I could not afford to miss. (Does insurance cover arrest as a reason for missing a flight?) Of course, I consented to my release, but with a slightly bad conscience. But I ensured representations were made to the Minister on behalf of the other two detainees.

As I left the police station, now as an honoured passenger of the police care that was awaiting me, one of the policemen who had administered the blows placed his hand over his heart and bowed low to me as I passed, gestures that I ever afterwards detested. The whirligig of time had brought in its revenges, and very swiftly too. The policeman who would gladly have beaten me moments before now feared for his job and thought he was in my power.

The question that ran through my mind during the whole episode was not what would happen to me but how I would describe it, and where.

This kind of dissociation from immediate experience is what helped educated people soon to take imprisonment in their stride. Certainly, it confirmed for me something I told patients who I thought were unhealthily self-obsessed: that it is more important to be able to lose yourself than to find yourself. The problem with this advice is that it provides no guidance as to how to lose yourself. The state of not being interested in anything other than yourself is a lamentable one, as Francis Bacon pointed out four hundred years ago. It is a poor centre of a man's actions, himself. Lamentation, however, is not the same as correction.

9

Rule Forty Five

I was surprised one day to find in the prison a young doctor as a prisoner. I asked him the reason for his imprisonment and he told me that he had downloaded and looked at some child pornography on the hospital computers. I told him at once that he was under no circumstances to confide what he had done to anyone else, for he would then be the object of violence by other prisoners. He should make up a simple story — something perfectly acceptable to prisoners, such as violence towards his wife — and stick to it. If his true offence ever became known, for example by revelation in the newspapers, or especially by television or radio, he might have to 'go on the rule' — that is to say Rule Forty Five (once more euphoniously rule Forty Three) according to which a prisoner under threat could apply to be protected from other prisoners by being lodged on a separate wing of the prison. This was not granted automatically, but only with the permission of a senior member of staff.

The doctor claimed that he had downloaded the pictures

only from curiosity and, because of a feeling of professional solidarity, I wanted to believe him.

Whether his offence should have been criminal is not a straightforward question, the main argument for it being so is that without demand there would be no supply. I was once involved as a witness in a case that dramatically supported this argument.

The police arrived at my room in the hospital one day and asked whether I would look at some appalling videos of sexual abuse of children by their parents. They came from a distant police district and for some reason they wanted an opinion from far away. There were thirty hours of these videos, they said, and they warned me that some of the officers who had sat through them were so disturbed by them that they had to take time off work afterwards. They were by no means the kind of people to shrivel at the first sign of unpleasantness.

The case was this. A married couple in a small and unremarkable town had been caught sending films of the grossest abuse — torture, really — of their own children to subscribers on the internet. In those days when transmission was much slower than it is today, suspicion had been aroused by the size of their telephone bills, which were of higher order of magnitude or two from those of their neighbours.

The couple had constructed a sexual torture-chamber in their house which from the outside was like a thousand others. The chamber was positively mediaeval. In the event, it was necessary for me to watch only a few of minutes of the videos to answer the question to which the police wanted an answer.

The parents suspended their daughters upside down from chains attached to the ceiling. The mother, herself naked, would then beat them with what looked like long, thin flexible branches of trees, shouting at them that they were wicked, deserved what they were getting, and asking them whether they wanted to be good from then onwards. She would take a dildo and rape them repeatedly. Pouring scorn on them for enjoying it so much. The children remained silent throughout, which was more sinister than if they and cried out in pain. It was as if this treatment were routine for them — which it was.

Apparently, people paid £1000 for access to such a video.

It was the husband who filmed the proceedings and who claimed, after his arrest, that his wife was not just acting under his orders but under pharmacological control. The husband claimed that he gave his wife a dose of morphine before each episode and that this turned her into an automaton with no will of her own.

As such, of course, she could be guilty of no crime. The police wanted to exclude this as a possible defence and after only a few minutes (even less, in fact, even before they showed me the video), I was able to provide them with an assurance that the attempted exculpation was absurd, pharmacological nonsense.

It was evident that the woman was a full participant in the torture of her own children and was in a state of high excitation during it. I furnished the police with a report of a few lines, and no more was ever heard of this defence.

Oddly enough, though, the woman was given a much lighter sentence than the man. I never knew the full details of the case but knew enough to find this difference more than surprising. Whatever the precise allocation of the responsibility between them, she was bad enough to have been given the maximum sentence, even if it were the same as that of her husband, who was the guiltier of the two. There is necessarily a maximal severity, a level above which the punishment cannot be proportional, even approximately, to the guilt of the parties involved. Had I not seen the video with my own eyes, I should not have believed that such treatment of children by their parents were possible.

But had there been no demand for such videos, would they have behaved in this way? What would they have been like as parents otherwise? And how had they gone about mounting their enterprise, finding their customers and so forth? I was never afterwards able to look at the façade of a seemingly respectable house such as theirs without wondering what was going on deep within it.

Prisoners accused of sex crimes were regarded by other prisoners as fair game for assault, the showers being a particularly dangerous place because supervision by officers was less close there and a beating could be administered very quickly by a gang falling upon their chosen victim. The victim could be slashed, either with a razor or other sharp object. One particular form of slashing that was used was called 'tramlining'. The prisoners would melt two blades of a razor into the plastic handle of a toothbrush and then draw it across a man's face. The resulting injury was not dangerous but it was disfiguring, since the two close parallel cuts made it impossible to repair them and therefore left a prominent scar of a certain easily recognisable type. Several times an officer asked me to attend to a prison who had just been 'tramlined.'

One heard rumours occasionally that the officers turned a blind eye to an attack on someone whom they abominated, but (perhaps not surprisingly) I never had any evidence of it.

As far as prisoners were concerned, anyone accused of a sex crime and remanded into custody was guilty. There was none of this nonsense, as they saw it, about innocence until guilt was proved. And a man who had asked for protection under Rule Forty Five was assumed to be a sex criminal. Just as in obstetrics there used to be a saying, once a Caesar always a Caesar (if a woman once gave birth by Caesarean section, any future child would have to be born the same way) so in prison there was a saying, once on the Rule, always on the Rule. In other words, the prisoners' institutional memory was long and their informal network of information strong. No prisoner on returning to prison, even after many years, could long hide the fact from other prisoners that he had once been on the rule.

Moreover, the information that a man had been on the rule seeped out of prison to the neighbourhood in which he lived, whose prevailing values and ethos were very like those of prison itself. Indeed, those neighbourhoods were in effect prisons without walls or prison officers, and prisons in which prison officers are not in control are, as any prisoner will tell you (though somewhat shamefacedly, for it undermines the conceit that prisoners and prison officers are mortal enemies — them and us), by far the worst and most violent.

I remember a prisoner who was charged with the rape of two young women. He was no stranger to prison but had never been charged with such a crime before and he strenuously denied it. His name and photograph had been prominently published in his local newspaper. At his trial, however, not only did the prosecution fail to prove his guilt, but — what was more unusual — the defence proved his innocence beyond all reasonable doubt. His two accusers were arrested and subsequently sent to prison.

He told me before the trial, though, that even if he were acquitted, as he believed that he would be, he would not be able to return to where he had been living for many years. Mere innocence would not protect him from the attacks of his neighbours. The windows of his house had already been smashed and he would have to move away to another part of the country altogether, where he was not known, if he were to have any peace.

Justice is fragile and the desire for it by no means natural or universal. 'Love of justice in most men,' said La Rochefoucauld, 'is only fear of suffering injustice.' There are few more gratifying states of mind than moral outrage and when this can be allied with the joys of destructiveness, as for example in the breaking of windows, something like ecstasy is reached, especially when in communion with like-minded (or like-inflamed) others. Often the moral indignation is what Freud called projection, the ascription to others of what one had done, felt, desired or brought about.

Of nowhere is this more true than in contemporary England. When a notorious paedophile is taken to court, an angry crowd, or mob, often gathers to howl at him as he arrives. They give the impression that they would gladly tear him limb from limb if they could. Mothers with a child in tow often scream and wave their fists at the vehicle in which the accused arrives, and in the process terrify the child.

Curiously enough, none of the mothers sees this as a kind of child abuse. Nor does she reflect that her own path through life, as often as not, had been propitious for the spread of child abuse.

One day a prisoner came to me demanding Valium. I asked him why he needed it. 'If you don't give it to me, he said, 'I'll have to attack a nonce.' A 'nonce' is prison slang for a sex offender. The term does not appear in Partridge's dictionary of 1949 either, so its origin is comparatively recent. The claimed etymological derivation of the word, that it is short for nonsense, seems unlikely to me, given its extreme emotional charge.

'Why will you have to attack a nonce?' I asked.

'They interfere with little kiddies, don't they?'

'As a matter of fact, not all of them,' I said. As any textbook will demonstrate, they differ quite widely.

'Well anyway,' he said, 'I'll have to attack one of them if you don't give me no Valium.' I couldn't help recalling the late Tommy Cooper's joke. A man goes to his doctor and says, 'I need some sleeping tablets for my wife.' The doctor asks why? 'Because she woke up.'

He did indeed look quite agitated. I had been in the situation before in which a prisoner said he would commit an act of serious violence if I did not prescribe Valium for him.

One, for example, said to me:

'I'll kill someone if I don't give me nothing.' In the context, something could only mean Valium.

'Let me give you some advice,' I said.

'What is it?'

'Don't kill anyone.'

'You'll see', he said. 'You'll be sorry. It'll be down to you. It'll be your fault. You won't be able to sleep at night.'

The only reason he gave for wanting to kill someone was that he felt like it. In fact, he often felt like it. There was the petulance in his voice of a child denied what he wants — though as he stomped out I could not be absolutely certain that he would not carry out his threat. He was, after all, in prison for a violent offence.

While I was certain that if he did kill someone it would be his own moral responsibility and not mine, this is increasingly not the view of society. Two recent cases illustrate a worldwide trend to regard experts and officials as being permanently *in loco parentis*, the children being the entire adult population.

In Japan a man aged twenty six slaughtered nineteen handicapped people and injured twenty five others. Not long before he had told a psychiatrist what he wanted to do, but the psychiatrist left him at liberty and is now held to blame, popularly if not legally. And in France a judge released a young man from prison who had twice tried to go to Syria to join the jihadists, who then cut the throat of an eighty-six-year-old priest as a he was saying mass. In the ensuing furore, the possibility that the judge might only have been complying with what he thought were the requirements of the law was completely lost from view. It might as well have been he who cut the throat of the poor priest for all the opprobrium he received.

But errors of prediction — in both directions, too gloomy and too optimistic — are inevitable. Where judgement has to be exercised it will often be mistaken (the error in the French case, if there was one, was in the original sentencing).

The prisoner who said that he would kill someone if I did not prescribe Valium did not kill anyone or even, as far as I know, commit any act of violence. His was a simple attempt at blackmail. But if he had been in earnest I should have been severely blamed. As it was, I preserved my reputation as someone who could not, in local prison parlance, be 'blagged' into prescribing.

To return to the man who said he would have to kill a nonce (if I did not prescribe), I asked him whether he had any children himself.

'Three', he said.

'Same mother?' I asked.

'Three', he said.

'And do you see the children?'

'No.'

'Why not?'

'The new boyfriends,' he said.

'And do you think these are the last boyfriends the mothers will ever have, or will they have more than one?'

'More than one.'

'And how will one or more of those boyfriends treat your children?'

He grasped the implication at once. Strangely enough he did not grow angry.

'I don't think, then, that you ought to attack a nonce because he interferes with little kiddies. You haven't abused your children yourself, but you've maximised the chances of them being abused.'

He left the room in a calmer frame of mind than he

entered it and I never heard that he had attacked any other prisoner. The speed with which he had grasped the point suggested to me again that the mental capacities of prisoners were often greater than commonly supposed. Nor did they commit crimes, as Luther stood at the Diet of Worms, because they could do no other.

Prisoners on the Rule had a special wing in which the average age was very much higher than 'on normal location'. There it was not uncommon to find an old man who walked with a stick, whether he needed one or not. I suppose they wanted to create a maximum aura of vulnerability — rather than that of invulnerability desired elsewhere in the prison — to obtain the maximum protection. Who would be so cowardly as to attack an old man who needed a stick?

Some proclaimed their innocence and said they were the victims of conspiracy. They had often been accused many years after their alleged offences by a group of accusers who stood to be awarded compensation if the charges against him were, if not proved, at least believed (compensation paid, of course, mostly by the taxpayer).

The similarity of the accusers' stories was taken as some kind of corroboration, but this sometimes seemed to me a little like buying several copies of the same newspaper to find out whether what was written in it was true. On the other hand, terrible abuse went on and presumably had always gone on. I pitied the poor juries who had to decide in such cases. Not to be believed when the accusation was true was to double the harm done by the crime; but to be convicted when innocent, and to be treated ever after as guilty, was terrible too.

Occasionally I would meet prisoners who had been convicted of what in America is called, with laudable economy, 'statutory rape', that is to say of having had sexual relations with a minor below the age of consent.

Their stories were always the same (which, of course, didn't make them true). They never denied that they were guilty in the technical sense, but the girls were always mature for their age and led the man on without informing him of her age; it is not usual in sexual encounters to demand a birth certificate. The relationship would continue happily for a time but, as was inevitable, would end. It was then that the girl would either inform on the man or, if her parents were already aware of what was going on (which was often the case), complain about him. He would be convicted in effect not for having had sex with the girl, but for having stopped having sex with her.

Where the men claimed that the parents were aware of what was going on, they were held by the prisoners to be equally guilty and therefore experienced their punishment as unjust.

What could be said in defence of these men? It is certainly true that children, particularly girls, reach physical maturity much earlier than they once did. The average age of menarche is said to have declined by a year every decade for the last three decades, as average height has increased by an inch per decade. Some publications for girls aged twelve are largely about how to make themselves sexually attractive. It is true also that many British girls look on their release for the day from school as if their ambition is to be a prostitute as soon as possible.

And those parents I have interviewed who were complicit in their child's illegal sexual relation with an older man always use the same arguments as to why they did not put an end to it. The first is that they cannot stop them. It is an argument that is not without some force, though it does not explain why they do not denounce the man.

I remember a patient who took an overdose because he was threatened with imprisonment if he did not get his fifteen-year-old daughter to stop playing truant from school. But what, he asked, was he supposed to do? Deposit her by force at the school entrance and stand guard to ensure that she did not leave? If he so much as laid a finger on her she might accuse him of assault; and I have met not a few adolescents who are fully aware of the legal prohibition on force and used it to defy their parents. It might be said that his daughter's defiance of his authority was his own fault, that she was as he and her mother had made her. While this might have been true in many cases of such defiance, it was not true in all. Fractious, difficult children are born as well as made; there are children who would be defiant even if parents assiduously followed all the advice of Dr Benjamin Spock, or whoever is the modern equivalent of that now-forgotten figure. I had the impression that the distress of this father was not just caused by the possibility imprisonment (remote, I think, for I never saw a prisoner imprisoned for such an offence), but from the sheer frustration caused him by his petulant, disobedient daughter. He was of the white-working class and so could safely be persecuted by the authorities. I saw many Moslem girls who had been prevented by their fathers from attending school when legally obliged to do so, and never once did I hear of their authorities intervening, despite the girls' — burning — desire to attend school.

The other argument employed by parents who connived at the illegal sexual intercourse of their daughters with older men was that the age of consent (sixteen) was absurd. They did not argue that, children maturing much earlier these day, the age of consent should be lowered, say to fourteen; or that the sensible Italian law should be adopted lowering the age of consent, but for consenting adolescents. Instead, without quite realising it, they argued for the abolition of an age of consent at all, for it was absurd, they said, to suppose that a girl was mature enough to consent to sexual relations on her sixteenth birthday but not mature enough the day before. This argument, of course, could have been applied to any age of consent whatsoever, for such maturity never arrives from one day to the next.

It struck me then that our society is increasingly one in which people will not accept arbitrary limits, or at any rate limits that are inevitably to some extent arbitrary, in so far as they cannot be syllogistically derived from indisputable first principles, as the 'correct' age for consent cannot ever be. Only limits, if any, that they set themselves are acceptable to them. They are the arbiters of everything. Individualism can scarcely go further.

Oddly enough, this ideological and often practical liberalism goes along with a vicious censoriousness which is often expressed in violence, as it is expressed in prison — or would be, if the officers did not keep order.

It is difficult not to conclude that in Britain the hysterical fear of paedophilia is not a distorted expression of guilt about the way many of the British now bring up their children, that is to say with a mixture of neglect, overindulgence and violence. Surveys of the kind in which I do not usually put much faith repeatedly show that children are the least happy and most anxiety-ridden in Europe, and I think it is possibly easy to observe why this should be.

Were the men accused or convicted of statutory rape telling the truth, and if they were, did it matter? The fact is that men who molested girls as young as six or seven also claimed to have been led on by them, as if it were the children who were the adults and the adults who were the children.

Not all the prisoners on the Rule were sex-offenders, however. Some were seeking protection from other prisoners who had threatened them, or were known or suspected to be grasses, or were former policemen or prison officers.

They did not attack the nonces and peace reigned between them. The contemptuous enmity of other prisoners served as social cement, just as the classical French sociologist, Durkheim would have predicted, for they felt under siege all the time and knew that if protection were withdrawn they would be immediately attacked and perhaps even killed.

This meant that the Protection Wing, as it was known, was the calmest, quietest and in some sense the most civilised wing in the prison. There was none of the shouting, the willing embrace of noise, on the Protection Wing, which made it a comparative pleasure to walk through. There were never any fights and the inmates were invariably polite, even ingratiating. In part this was because their offences, on average, were committed when they were older; they were of rather higher social class also; but mainly it was because of the substratum of fear on which their lives in prison rested. That fear would never leave them.

Not that it would prevent them from re-offending, though.

On one notable occasion, however, a sex-offender received the kindest treatment from other prisoners. He was a small and slight creature of very peculiar appearance and of such low intelligence that he could barely speak. He had, apparently, assaulted a woman sexually by trying to feel her up.

It was immediately obvious that he had no understanding of why he had been incarcerated, nor any capacity to adapt to these unfamiliar and frightening surroundings. He did not know, and could not learn, where he was or why. He was admitted at once to the hospital wing where his howls of distress still ring in my ears. It was pitiful, and outrageous that he had been sent here, but there was no other institution ready or willing to take him. The prison was under legal obligation to accept whoever was sent.

The other prisoners on the hospital wing did not react to him as they would have reacted to an ordinary nonce. If one of the latter had ever to be admitted to the hospital wing, he had to remain under special protection, it being a fundamental human need to have someone to look down on.

On the contrary, they recognised at once that his case was different, and they looked after him with what can only be called tender solicitude. Under their care his howling ceased and he became almost happy; more interestingly, perhaps, the prisoners who looked after him became happier too. They had found a purpose in life — necessarily a temporary one — and were aware of doing good, no doubt a new sensation for some of them.

After about two weeks, a more suitable place was found for this young man, but he could not have been better looked after there than he had been by the prisoners. They were sad to see him go; he had briefly enabled the prisoners to express normal human kindness without it being taken as a sign of weakness and therefore of exploitability. Whatever the state of their feelings, prisoners must at all times exhibit a hard carapace to their fellows if they want to avoid victimisation; but except for the genuinely hard-hearted and psychopathic (a minority), the pose, often equally necessary in the social environment from which they came outside of prison, exerted a strain. The young man with his need for care came as a relief to them.

The degree to which so many of the prisoners came from a radically loveless world, in which all human relationships were struggles for power, control and advantage, did not so much shock as sadden me. They came from a world in which there was no *savoir vivre* at all: only the coarsest appetites and crudest satisfactions counted or were known to them.

It was surprising, in a way, that prisoners were not worse than they were; and an optimist (which I am not) might take the fact that they were not worse than they were as proof that man is not fundamentally bad, but only made so by society. It is true that they had often had childhoods that were of a willful cruelty (and stupidity) that surpassed understanding. That cruelty was often joyful for the person who committed it.

One day a prisoner who had been imprisoned several times for burglary came to me and asked me whether I thought that his continual resort to burglary had something to do with his childhood.

'Absolutely nothing whatever', I replied. I never encouraged prisoners to ascribe their criminal acts directly to their childhoods, in the manner of one billiard ball (their childhood) striking another (them).

This answer took him aback.

'Why do I do it, then?', he asked.

'Because,' I replied, 'you're lazy and stupid and want things that you won't work for.'

Far from becoming angry, as one might have expected, he laughed. I think my straighter-than-straight talking came almost as a relief, as if he had no longer to play a difficult assigned role. It is not easy to keep up a part, at least until it has become so second nature that it is no longer a part.

Once over the play-acting, it was possible to talk to him honestly about his childhood which, though it had not caused him to break into people's houses and carry away valuables as low temperature causes water to freeze, was still a matter of genuine distress to him.

Of course, one had to be careful whom one treated in this no-nonsense way. Some prisoners were so well-defended, as psychotherapists put it, against the assault of truth that they would explode if spoken to in this way. The art was to spot them beforehand.

Another burglar came to me shortly after having been sentenced to yet another term of imprisonment. He gave every appearance of being angry.

'Prison's no use to me,' he said. 'Prison's not what I need. I don't need prison.'

'What do you need?' I asked.

'I need 'elp', he said.

'Help with what?'

'Help to stop me burgling.'

'I'm not sure there is such help', I said.

'Prison's no use to me.'

'But it is to me', I said.

'What do you mean?' he asked, looking puzzled.

'Well, as a householder I know that while you're inside, you're not burgling my house.'

He laughed, his anger, or pseudo-anger dissipated.

In fact, my answer, that his imprisonment was of use to me, could have been interpreted differently.

Though I was not well-paid by comparison with work I could have done elsewhere (it more than halved my ultimate pension), I *was* paid. And it was not really my house the prisoner was likely to have burgled if he had been at liberty, for if he were a typical burglar he would have burgled houses very near to where he lived and very like his own. It is often forgotten — I would say almost always forgotten — that, if the majority of criminals are poor, the great majority of their victims are likewise poor. Since the class of victim is very much larger than that of perpetrator, each perpetrator committing on average many crimes a year, lenience towards criminals is not tantamount to tenderness towards the poor.

I met more than one 'ethical' burglar in prison, or burglars who considered themselves such. The first said he broke only into rich people's houses, and stole only antiques.

'They can afford it,' he said. 'They're insured. They can replace them.'

'But perhaps they're attached to the ones they have', I said. 'Heirlooms are of sentimental value.' Of the misery caused by the violation of one's home I did not speak. But the 'ethical' burglar would not have it. If you have enough money to replace something, then you could not really miss it.

I discovered that he himself had come to like and value antiques. His taste had developed with his 'work,' like that of any dealer in antiques, I suppose. His flat, rather unusually for the area in which he lived, was furnished with the pieces he particularly liked.

'I daresay your girlfriend will sell them while you're in here', I said. He frowned and looked furious.

'She'd better not,' he said.

'Why?' I asked. 'You can replace them.'

'I'd break her f.....g legs!'

Another 'ethical' burglar told me that he would never steal from an old lady or a child. If he knew that there was one of those in a house, he would not break in. This entailed of course reconnaissance and planning on his part, while most burglary is opportunistic. An open window draws the burglar in as a magnet draws iron filing. If by chance he made a mistake and discovered that there was an old lady or child in the house he was breaking into, he retired from it without having taken anything — a professional burglar's gallantry.

Of course not all the burglars I met were gallant, far from it. One burglar, whom I had previously seen in my clinic in the hospital next door, had been a glue-sniffer from an early age. When not on the glue, as it were, he was pleasant enough, though still light-fingered. One day he took the dictaphone from my desk and I called hospital security (I remember the days when such a department in a hospital was unimaginable as being necessary), who in turn called the police.

A few days later I received through the post a standard letter asking me whether I would like 'victim support', as though I were so fragile psychologically that the loss of a dictaphone to theft would disequilibrate me. I thanked the police for their solicitude, but said that I had not been deeply attached to the piece of equipment (the hospital's incidentally, not mine).

Nor did I expect the police to make gargantuan efforts to catch the thief: I wanted only for the police to record the crime so that their statistics would reflect reality slightly more accurately. A lot of mental effort, after all, goes into manipulating the statistics, mainly downwards. Unexpectedly, it would have been as well had the police made such gargantuan efforts.

A few weeks later the thief returned to the hospital 'high' on glue. Demanding a prescription, he threatened a distinguished physician and pinned him for a time against a corridor wall. Then he ran off. Two days later, again under the influence of glue, he broke into a very old man's house and brutally beat him to death.

I saw the culprit the next day in the prison. His remorse was less than overwhelming. He was more concerned with the arrival of his 'canteen', the small luxuries amongst which prisoners were allowed to choose once a week (and for which they had to pay from their allowance), and his 'smoker's pack', the tobacco which every prisoner was given on reception into prison on the very nearly correct assumption that all criminals smoked, than with the seriousness of his crime.

Tobacco for prisoners was regarded, also very nearly, as a human right rather than as an object of prohibition for their own good. The weaker brethren were often relieved of their ration while the officers had to be asked for the gift of a light (addressed as 'Boss' or 'Guv'). This gave the more sadistically-inclined among them an easy way to frustrate the prisoners, telling them that they would give them a light in due course and then making them wait for it when there had been nothing to prevent them from giving it straight away.

When a man is locked up he either thinks about the meaning of life or, more frequently, dwells on his petty frustrations and stews in the juice of resentment, magnifying small wrongs into justifications for future bad actions. I quite often saw prisoners made to wait for something for no apparent reason other than the desire to frustrate them.

> But man, proud man,
> Dress'd in a little brief authority

No longer under the influence of glue, the man who the day before had bludgeoned an old man to death was now preoccupied by the non-arrival of his tobacco, experiencing it as an injustice and infringement of his rights.

For a time, violence in the hospital next door to the prison became so serious a problem that a police station located in it supplemented the security department. This, if anything, made matters worse, for it convinced wrong-doers that they had nothing to fear from the boys (and girls) in blue. The latter resolutely refused to take action even against those whom they witnessed personally acting in an aggressive or violent way. It was as if they were under orders to keep the statistics down — the prevention of a rise in the figures, rather than in crime, being their main responsibility. Sir Robert Peel would have turned in his grave.

The final straw for me came when a nurse in the casualty department told me that she had been punched in the face by a patient in front of a policeman who had done nothing except preventing the patient from repeating his action. He had not arrested him, let along charged him.

I wrote a letter to the Chief Constable of the city to complain of the supine nature of his force, and described the case of the nurse.

He relied assuring me that his officers were under strict instruction to arrest and charge every violent offender in the hospital. In effect, he said that what had happened could not have happened. The nurse was lying or psychotic perhaps.

I did not believe that the nurse was lying, but of course could not have stood in a court of law and say that I knew for a fact that what she told me was true. Against an administrative blockade there is very little that the ordinary citizen can do, unless he turns himself into a militant campaigner.

Nevertheless, my letter to the Chief Constable bore fruit (of a kind), though likewise I cannot absolutely swear to cause and effect. About three months later police posters began to appear throughout the hospital informing the public that any person who assaulted a member of staff within the hospital premises would be arrested and charged.

I took this as an indication that my original complaint had been justified. But also that on the facts above the Chief Constable was an unscrupulous liar, more a politician than a policeman. He had an eye more to pleasing his masters than to the protection of the public — something common to practically all Chief Constables nowadays, for whom pre-empting criticism is more important than pre-empting crime.

The police posters, while better than nothing, perhaps, were unsatisfactory (though revealing), nonetheless. They expressed the idea that the response to the crime of assault depended upon who assaulted whom, as well as where the assault took place. Hospital; staff, like the rest of the population, were fair game again once they left the hospital premises.

No doubt the framer of the poster did not really mean to imply this, nor was it literally true in all cases. But certainly the will to prevent, repress and prosecute crime was less than of iron strength.

I first realised this (having returned from many years abroad) when I had a patient who had been the victim of what seemed to me — and seemed to her also — a very serious crime. I was by then in the peculiar situation of talking to the victims of crime (as many of my patients were) in the morning in hospital, and talking to the perpetrators of crime in the afternoon in the prison next door, when I had to control my natural prejudice against them in order to see them as individuals and not just as members of a despised or despicable class.

My patient was a woman in her fifties who served in a

small store in one of those bleak working-class housing estates of concrete tower blocks, the space between which served as wind-tunnels, and where notices on the grass warned children not to play on it (especially ball games) as the grass was an amenity to be enjoyed by everyone. Some of the amenities to be enjoyed by everyone were the underpasses which were enjoyed mainly by muggers and drug-dealers. The community centre, so-called, was a concrete block and bunker given a hideous shape by its designer as a reluctant concession to aesthetics.

I came to know these tower blocks well, with their freezing lobbies, wire-meshed windows, aluminium-lined lifts smelling of urine, and stairwells strewn with used needles and syringes, when I visited psychotic patients who used their own furniture as firewood on the upteenth floor because their electricity had been cut off for non-payment of bills, their Rastafarian neighbours making the whole building vibrate day and night with their music (I met two prisoners who had been charged with attempted murder because murder had been the only way to control the volume and persistence of music, polite requests and appeals to the housing authorities having failed completely, the authorities lacking all courage). I knew the tenants who complained of the black fungus attacking their walls in science-fiction quantities, and who met with blank denial from the housing authorities until I wrote a letter to the director of the city housing department (which never bothered to deal with anyone at a lower level); and the old ladies afraid to go out of their front doors and under permanent curfew imposed by the muggers; the curious characters who did not leave their flats on the upper floors except by abseiling down the building; the jealous men who dragged their supposedly errant lovers by their hair across the room, making a terrible noise for the tenants below; and the schizophrenics who spent their nights moving their furniture to blockade their flat against invaders and erected peculiar apparatus to deflect the rays that their neighbours were beaming in. They were the location of a modern *Satyricon*.

The store in which my patient served refused entry to the children of the local secondary school because they stole so much. With the agreement of the headmaster of the school, it was decreed off-limits to the pupils (or as we say these days, the 'students') of the school. One day, however, three boys aged fourteen, already the size of full-grown men of thirty years ago, entered the store.

'You know you're not allowed in here,' my patient said to them.

They took this not as a prohibition but as a challenge. One of them jumped over the counter and started to strangle my patient while the other two laughed as they filled their pockets. My patient felt she was going to die but the boy let go before she passed out. The boys then ran away and my patient called the police.

Rather unusually, the police caught the boys: they gave them an official warning. It was this that upset my patient. She felt her life had been in danger — from her description, it had been in danger, for stranglers often go farther than they intend — but the trivial punishment of the boys, not even rising to the level of a slap on the wrist, made her realise how little the state cared for her safety or even her life. She counted for nothing. Worse still she had seen the boys in the street and they had laughed at her, as well they might, for they thought they had achieved some kind of triumph over her. She did not return to work.

I respected policemen on the whole as individuals. Most of them wanted to do as good a job as they were able to, and most would unhesitatingly risk their lives to save a member of the public — if procedure allowed them to do so, of course. But as an organisation the police (except in such matters as the prevention of terrorism) were woeful. The Chief Constables were chosen for the smoothness rather than for the straightness of their talk. Their job consisted largely of putting obstacles in the way of their men. But in this they were only obeying orders.

One day I was called to a police station nearby to see a man who had been arrested who showed every sign of being mad. I parked my car on the street directly outside the station, from which it was clearly visible. While I was examining the man in the cells someone broke into the car (smashing a window) and stole its radio, as it was still easy to do at the time.

When I discovered this, I returned to the police station to report it. I remember to this day what the duty desk sergeant said to me:

'Oh, that'll be the Smiths from number 22. They're breaking into our cars all the time.'

After a brief pause to recover from what he said, I said:

'Why don't you do something about it? After all, you're the police.'

The desk sergeant shrugged. That was what life was like.

Another time, at the same police station, I witnessed how little some policemen cared for public safety by comparison with meeting the targets set by their superiors. I had been called to examine a man in the cells who had gone up to a woman waiting at a bus-stop and tried to chop her neck with a meat-cleaver. She had never seen him before, nor had he her; but as he hacked at her, he exclaimed 'Mary Queen of Scots was innocent, so you have to die as well.'

The logic of this was not at all clear. Fortunately the woman's clothing obstructed the cleaver and prevented injury, though there can have been few more terrifying experiences than this. The world would never seem a safe place to the victim again: any passer-by might carry a fatal weapon and attack with no reason.

I examined the man in the police cells — he was clearly mad. He was in a world of his own that had little in common with the ordinary world. It was impossible to follow what he was saying. One thought did not connect with another and however hard you delved, you never reached a coherent explanation of what he had done. It was as if he had a private language, the language that Wittgenstein denied could exist.

I told the custody sergeant that the man was mad, which hardly came as news to him. I suggested that he charge the man with attempted murder. After all, he had made clear his intent to kill. I did not, of course, think that he could or should be found guilty of such a crime (unless his madness were the result of involuntary intoxication with drugs, which further tests and observation might establish). But there ought to be a proper legal record of his very dangerous act, and a trial, which would result in his admission to hospital under strict supervision. This would not only protect the public, but go some way to reassure the victim that the matter was being taken seriously.

The custody sergeant, who clearly wanted to disembarrass himself of the lunatic as quickly as possible, insisted that he could not legally charge a madman and that if I did not take him immediately to hospital without a charge being laid against him, he, the custody sergeant, would have to release him back on to the streets and even give him back his cleaver, as it was his property (so far as he knew).

This was blackmail, but in vain did I argue with him. I said that if the man had actually succeeded in killing the woman he would not have said that he could not charge him and let him on to the street if he were not taken at once to hospital without a charge. The case was no different now, I said; moreover, our hospital was not secure, there were no locked doors, and it was easy to escape from it. Surely public safety required that he keep the man until some suitable place be found for him? The custody sergeant was adamant. Either I admitted him to hospital immediately or he would release him. I judged that he meant what he said and that he was prepared to release the man back on to the streets and I felt obliged to concede.

There is therefore no public record of this event. No crime had been committed; and the victim must have been left long in a kind of limbo wondering what became of the man who had tried to kill her for no reason — or for a mad reason.

The police had several other methods of reducing the crime rate and of clearing up crimes to no one's benefit but their own. I once had a patient, a young man of Indian descent, who had just left university with a first-class degree in a subject that guaranteed him an excellent job. He had a couple of weeks to fill before he took up his first post and he spent them helping his parents in their shop — a small grocery that had, as with so many Indian immigrants, been the material means of the social ascent of the next generation.

He was serving alone in the shop when three young louts, well known in the area and to the police, entered. They began to take beer from the fridge and my patient, believing them to be under-age, asked for identification. They left the shop, beer in hand.

He followed them to just outside the door and told them to return the beers. One of them turned on him and swung a punch, missing him but instead hitting the shopfront window, seriously gashing his forearm which started to bleed copiously. The two associates ran away, but my patient told the young man to come back into the shop, where he stemmed the bleeding and called an ambulance. He also called the police.

The latter not surprisingly managed to find the two other miscreants and charged all three with theft, as well as one of them with attempted assault. But then the three of them, each with a long criminal record despite their youth, alleged that my patient had run out of the shop and assaulted *them*. The police affected to believe that this preposterous story and arrested my patient. They persisted in charging him, and the prosecuting authorities planned a trial. They said they would drop the charges only if he dropped the charges against the three louts.

No doubt there have been worse injustices in the history of the world, but it would be difficult for my patient ever again to believe in the justice of the British criminal justice system. Unfair trials are not the only way for injustice to be done.

10

The Thin Blue Squiggle

My wife experienced the willful incompetence and moral degradation of the police herself. We had just retired and were about to move house. We had a skip in our front garden near to the house in which we placed the solid and bulky rubbish that every household accumulates and which we did not want to take with us to our new house. My wife looked out of the window and saw some youths setting fire to the contents of the skip. She called the police and they asked her what she wanted them to do.

'I want you to arrest them, of course,' she said.

That was impossible: the police were busy elsewhere. My wife said that in that case she wanted a crime number so that at least the crime was recorded. To this proposal the police put up fierce resistance, refusing point blank at first. My wife insisted with some force. Eventually, they conceded and with much reluctance recorded the crime. It spoiled their figures, both by increasing the numbers of crimes and reducing the ratio of those that were solved. That was not the end of the matter. A few minutes later a senior policeman, high up in the hierarchy, phoned my wife to tell her that she had been wasting police time by her complaint.

I was very angry when I heard this and wrote what an old-fashioned Indian acquaintance of mine, a distinguished doctor, called a stinker to the Chief Constable to demand an apology and a reprimand of the senior policeman who had time to upbraid my wife but not to apprehend arsonists. As is so often the case, sloth, or other employments, overcame rage and I let it pass. It is wrong, of course, to write while angry, but when anger has dissipated the letter does not get written.

I did once write an article about the inertia of the police, however, in a newspaper of large circulation. It aroused the Chief Constable of a distant constabulary to write a reply. He said that it took four hours nowadays to process an arrest, that is to say half of a policeman's shift, and I wouldn't want there to be no policemen patrolling the streets because they were all filling in forms. I believe the post-arrest process is still lengthening.

The utterly defeatist tone of his letter was obvious. The Chief Constable took the length of the police's administrative tasks for granted, as if it was a raw fact about the universe and could no more be changed than could the law of gravity. I am fully aware of the difficulty in reducing administrative procedure once it has been introduced, of course. (I have even suggested a small law of administration, namely that once it reaches a certain critical level all attempts to reduce it increase it.) Nevertheless, it appeared dispiriting that a senior policeman should consider the apprehension of criminals a waste of time.

The administrative procedures on which staff in all public services now spend so much of their time are simultaneously a means of work-creation and work-avoidance: the latter two being an instance of what the dialectical materialists used to call a dialectical unity. The procedures require the expenditure of time and effort while preventing or obstructing the pursuit of the ostensible goal of the whole organisation.

Occasionally, however, the inertia of the police can be defeated by a determined citizen, such as a near neighbour of ours. She was a retired university teacher in our residential area in Birmingham with Victorian houses.

Suddenly the area was invaded by street prostitutes (or 'sex-workers', as the medical journals now call them, the correct term for pimps not having been decided yet— 'brief sexual encounter facilitators'?). They were bussed in from another town every night. Dressed in cheap and flimsy but flashy finery, they were not all in the first flush of youth, far from it, and they were kept slim by a diet of cigarettes and cocaine. Close up they looked raddled and worn-out, but the street lighting — very old-fashioned lamps — was forgiving. Their customers, or whatever they should be called, were mainly commercial travellers from the nearby hotels. Sex took place in the backs of cars or against the niched walls of the church, and in the morning our rosebushes were sometimes draped with used condoms.

The latter were distributed, free of charge, to the prostitutes by the council from a white van which circled the area like a kerb-crawler, looking for harm to prevent. The van also distributed coffee and solid refreshment to the prostitutes, to help them in their work. Certainly the professional flimsiness of their costume must have caused them to feel cold in inclement weather. From the point of view of business, winter, with its short days and early darkness, was the best season.

Our neighbour, whom one might have thought had emerged from a novel by Barbara Pym, proved to have a backbone of granite as well as an eye of steel. She did not accept the situation fatalistically, as most of us did. In her seventies, she dragooned the local householders into a patrol of vigilantes who took down the customers' car registration numbers. This had a depressing effect upon business and one day the brief-sexual-encounter co-ordinator sat menacingly in his car as a counter to the vigilantes. I think he knew who his real enemy was, and when she approached the car he drew a gun. She was not impressed.

'Don't be so silly,' she said. 'Put that thing away.'

He did as he was told and retired, defeated. He had no intention of going to prison for murder.

My neighbour did not rest on her laurels, however, and next tackled the police. She went to the local station to complain that they were doing nothing to clear the streets of the prostitutes. The senior policeman at the station replied that the girls were already victims enough and he did not propose to make their lives worse or more difficult. This did not impress my neighbour either; she put her hand on the desk and said, 'That is not the law.'

The senior policeman realised at once that he had a redoubtable and dangerous opponent who would not accept inaction. One good quality of careerists, or quality that can be turned to account, is that they are acutely and almost instinctively aware of which opponent is serious and can harm them. The girls, as he called them, were swiftly moved on by his men to an area in which they would hardly be noticed, or if noticed not much disliked.

I had learned from dealing with bureaucracies on behalf of my patients whose verbal skills were such that they were reduced by the obstructionism of officialdom either to silence or to violence, with not much in between the two. They did not know how to write a letter or to whom. As for telephone calls, these could always be disavowed by officials, whose first line of defence in their struggle to do nothing was deny that they had any knowledge of the person calling them for the second, third or umpteenth time.

It was unsurprising, therefore, that when officials in offices had to come face to face with members of their public (their vassals, in some sort), they were often separated from them by a screen of reinforced and even bullet-proof glass. Visits to prison were more personal. I therefore never communicated with anyone below the highest administrative level, making clear, on behalf of my patients, that I would not desist until what they wanted or needed had been done. This method worked, at least for my patients, though I could see it was no way to run a system and might delay the solution of other, equally urgent problems. (This assumes, of course, that the time freed from dealing with my cases would have been spent on dealing with other cases — an assumption and no more than that.)

I do not want to give the impression that the police were uniformly lazy or careerist. On many occasions I was impressed by their bravery and devotion to duty, and the detectives in serious cases were remarkable for their persistence and determination, and — yes, intelligence. It was far from easy to outwit them, once they took up a case.

As a corporate body, though, the police had been emasculated and had lost that power of discretion which in a man of ill-will is dangerous but in a majority of cases is civilising. And the power of judgment is soon lost if not exercised.

The prison had a resident policeman who gathered intelligence and investigated crimes committed in the prison itself. He was in plain clothes, and I knew him to be a decent, intelligent and amusing man, possessed of a mordant sense of humour (which most policemen have, or used to have). One day he told me that he was resigning from the police and taking up a job with a private security firm. I asked him why.

'In the old days,' he said, 'we was nice to the nice people and nasty to the nasty people. Now we have to be nice to everyone.'

The strain had told. Administrative procedure is a perfect instrument for careerists but a demoralising burden for those who take the ostensible purpose of their jobs seriously, as a service as well as a career opportunity.

Nor do I wish to give the impression that the deformations I noticed in the police were unique to them — far from it. In the psychiatric services bureaucratically mandated incompetence also added to what was, no doubt, a natural tendency to it. The results were sometimes disastrous though, luckily, most incompetence went without disastrous effect.

It is often claimed that seventy per cent of prisoners have what are now called 'mental health issues'. I have even seen estimates as high as ninety per cent. These estimates, in my belief, are not only mistaken but bogus and intended to mislead.

The figures are intended to suggest that most prisoners are ill and ought to be in hospital — or that prison itself ought to be a kind of hospital. They insinuate both that current, decidedly untherapeutic, imprisonment is unjust, as well as that the psychiatric services ought to be almost indefinitely expanded to meet the needs for the poor criminals. They express an implicit deep belief in the efficacy of such services.

By comparison, the belief in the efficacy of miracle-working statues of the virgin is rational and well-founded. Is it really the case that for every human failing there is an equal and opposite therapy available as there is a Saint in the Catholic church?

Such surveys of prisoners fail to notice that psychiatric diagnosis has become so loose and all-encompassing, and the notion of mental health issues so limitless, that it would be possible to interpret the figure of seventy per cent as proving that prisoners are healthier than the general population.

When I added the maximum prevalence of all the disorders in the latest edition of the *Diagnostic and Statistical Manual of the American Psychiatric Association (DSM5)* — that organisation's great money-spinner upon which its survival now depends — I found that the average citizen of a western country would suffer from two and a half disorders a year. Prison, then, is an island of sanity.

The very notion of mental health is slippery and peculiar. Is it always to have healthy thoughts and emotions (whatever healthy thoughts are), to reason correctly, to desire only what is good for one, to be happy all the time, to be effective at work, never to lose one's temper, etc.? Is deviation from the norm inherently pathological, and do we not all sometimes deviate from the norm in some respect or other, often — but not always — to our own disadvantage?

Such statistics about the mental health of prisoners is what Freud, if he had been alive today, might have called a screen statistic. A screen memory, in his system of psychopathology, is a vivid and intrusive memory whose function is to hide and repress a much more disturbing memory that is thereby prevented from coming to consciousness. By analogy, a screen statistic is intended to prevent a worse or more scandalous reality from becoming known.

After all, if seventy per cent of prisoners have mental health issues (which means 'diagnosable disorders', according to the criteria laid down in *DSM5*), is it any wonder, and can it be the psychiatric services' fault that a relatively modest number of raving madmen languish untreated in prisons for lack of proper care? It is an interesting natural experiment on what raving madmen are like if left to their own devices. Give psychiatrists 'resources' and they will solve the job. But as the resources will never be sufficient to deal with seventy per cent of prisoners, the raving madmen will never be adequately treated. Conditions of eighteenth-century Bedlam will, therefore, continue until such time.

Once a man, who had seriously attacked an old woman in a churchyard without apparent reason, was remanded into prison and became my patient.

He did not attempt to rob her, which at least would have been a 'rational' reason for having attacked her. It was obvious from the first that he was mad; his vocalisations rarely rose to the level of words, let alone coherent sentences; he was dishevelled and neglected, so that he smelled horribly; he was enclosed in a world of his own, into which external stimuli seemed hardly to obtrude. He clearly responded to hallucinatory sounds, in all probability voices saying unpleasant or insulting things, or issuing strange orders. No doubt when he attacked the old lady he attributed some of the insults to her, which is why the attack would have made sense to him but not to her or to others.

In his cell in the prison hospital to which he had been allocated, he stripped naked and remained naked for the rest of his time in the prison. He was so preoccupied by his hallucinations that he seemed not to hear or see anyone who tried to speak to him: interlocutors did not exist for him.

His condition deteriorated. He hardly ate and lost weight steadily. He climbed on to his chair and shouted out of his window into the void beyond. The content of his expostulations, in so far as any was discernible at all, was religious in nature, a warning to the world that its end was nigh. Worst of all, and what was barely tolerable, was that he adorned the walls of his cell with religiose fragments of sentences painted in his own excrement.

This was not strictly what was called in prison as a 'dirty protest' (a term not appearing in Partridge either) in which a prisoner, usually psychopathic and always angered at a refusal to get his own way in some small matter or other — small things, as mentioned, loom large in prisoners' minds — smears his own faeces on the walls of his cell. Such protests became fewer in my time in the prison — at least such was my impression — perhaps, or probably, because the regime became more flexible and complaisant. But they did not cease altogether, and were a serious disciplinary offence. The dirty protester was taken 'down the block', or 'down the Seg' (that is to say the Segregation Unit), where prisoners were kept for a couple of days in solitary confinement as a punishment. The cell in which he had voiced (sic) his protest would then be cleaned by industrial cleaners in space-suits, using hoses of such power that the cells would soon be as new — or perhaps I should say as old.

But this prisoner in the hospital wing was not protesting. His was not a dirty protest, but rather a protestation of some kind of belief. We soon discovered that he was a psychiatric patient who had, in the explanatory or exculpatory phrase, 'slipped through the net.' When taking his medication he was, if not quite normal, at least not violent; but once he stopped taking it he became disordered in his thoughts and inclined to assault those whom he thought he heard insulting or threatening him. In other words, he thought his assaults were really self-defence.

There was a psychiatric team outside the prison that was supposed to care for patients such as he and to encourage him as far as possible to take his medication, often by fortnightly injection. When a patient was known either to neglect himself dangerously or attack others, or both, when not taking his medication, it could force him to do so.

I called the psychiatrist who had been in charge of this man's treatment outside the prison and asked him to take the patient into his hospital. This would necessitate visiting his patient and since delay is the small-arm of the administrator, he said he could not come for at least two weeks.

In the meantime, the situation became intolerable, though tolerated. The entire hospital smelled like a sewer, the man kept everyone awake at night with his incomprehensible exhortations to the world, he became thinner and thinner, and — to use an expression current in my childhood used to describe me when I had failed to comb my hair properly, which was often — he looked like the Wild Man of Borneo.

About two weeks after his admission to the hospital wing I arrived there after lunch to find two officers shaking their heads in bewilderment and disbelief. The man's psychiatrist had just left after visiting the man.

'What's wrong?' I asked.

'The doctor said, "it's just behaviour", Sir', said one of the officers.

'It's just behaviour', was what the officers said when they thought that bad conduct was the product of malignity rather than of madness.

'He said he's not mad, Sir', said the other officer. 'He says he's putting it on, acting.'

The man's condition continued to deteriorate. His psychiatrist had said that he would improve spontaneously once he realised that he was gaining nothing by his behaviour. After a further two weeks he agreed (by telephone) that this was unlikely, but that the prisoner's deterioration was only a mark of stubbornness. Then after another week he agreed that he was indeed unwell, but that, unfortunately, he had no hospital bed available for him. Here was scope for further prevarication.

Another week passed. I suggested that we go the whole hog and charge visitors to come and stare at him (baiting would be extra). I phoned a legal adviser as to whether, in view of the delay and the appalling conditions he had created for himself and others, I would be justified in treating him against his will, but he said that I could not, it would be against his human rights. Compulsory treatment were only possible if he had no capacity to decide for himself and it were a matter of life and death, which this was not. What about the rights of the other prisoners, I asked, and of the officers? Had they no right to peace and to breathe air that was not mephitic? Apparently not: human rights do not extend so far.

Eventually, exasperated by prevarication and procrastination, I asked the prison photographer to take photographs of the cell, which he did. The next day I phoned the psychiatrist yet again and told him that unless a bed was forthcoming for this man, I was sending the photographs to the Home Secretary himself next day, together with a verbal description of the cell, to ask whether he considered that prisoners ought to be kept in such conditions. A bed was found at once.

In defence of the psychiatrist, I am sure that he had few beds at his disposal because most of them had been closed down. He was therefore under intense pressure to tailor his diagnoses to his beds, rather than his beds to his diagnoses. The pressure of the beds transferred itself to pressure on intellectual and moral probity. The psychiatrist possibly had some version of the following false syllogism running through his mind:

> This man needs to be admitted to a hospital bed.
> There are no hospital beds.
> Therefore this man does not need to be admitted to a hospital bed.

The prison governor came to me after the man had been taken away to hospital.

'Did you have photographs taken of his cell?' he asked.

'Yes,' I replied. 'And I was going to send them to the Home Secretary.'

'That's completely forbidden, against the rules. Well done!'

I had great respect for this governor, the last and best whom I had known. Not for him to reprimand a man who, breaking the rules at risk to himself for the right result. He had come up through, unlike the others, so he knew every aspect of the job from the inside out. He was humane without being sentimental, had no illusions about human nature without being cynical, and could make a rule without it being worshipped as an idol. He was decidedly not:

> ... [a] bookful Blockhead, ignorantly read,
> With loads of learned lumber in his head,
> [who] With his own tongue still edifies his ears,
> And always listening to himself appears.

11

Recent Activity in Homicides

Shortly after my last day at the prison and hospital, I was asked to inquire into five murders committed by psychiatric patients (one followed by suicide), all within a small geographical area and within a short time. Were there any specific failings common to them in the way they had been treated that resulted in the tragic outcomes?

The inquiry presumed that such a cluster of rare events was not the work of chance. Subsequent statistical analysis, that I do not pretend to understand, demonstrated that, scientifically, the cluster could have been the work of chance, and that therefore there might be no lesson to be learned from it — assuming (what in my experience is doubtful) that anyone would learn such a lesson if it were there to be taught.

But it was too late. My two fellow-inquirers and I had already done our investigations. For me the lesson was as clear as day. In only one of the five cases had any of the staff taken a history of the patient (incidentally always called 'client' — despite frequent demonstrations that patients prefer to be called patients — because the word 'client' is less stigmatising; the kind of doublethink that is increasingly a prerequisite for a successful career in the National Health Service). There was no history in the hundreds of pages of notes on the other four cases, though taking the history is the most fundamental task in all clinical work.

In the one case in which a nurse actually took a history, she ignored its obvious import completely. It was as though she thought that the recording of the history was an end in itself, a religious ceremony propitiating goodness knows what god.

No history could have pointed to the terrible denouement, murder followed by suicide, more clearly. The man concerned had made a desperate suicide attempt before and could be persuaded only with great difficulty to go to hospital for life-saving treatment. There was every indication, both personal and statistical, that he was likely to commit suicide in the near future. Indeed, he said quite openly that such was his intention. The nurse had carefully recorded all this, and then concluded that he should be discharged at once from the hospital with no follow-up. Within twenty-four hours he had killed his wife and committed suicide, the latter by setting fire to himself.

The vast majority of the documentation in the other cases consisted of what were called 'Risk Assessment Forms'. They had been filled out hundreds of times.

The same questions — yes or no — were answered by tick or cross on each form. But it was difficult to believe that on each occasion the patient had actually been asked the questions. They would have driven him mad if they had. What most struck me about the forms, however, other than their huge number, was that the ticks and crosses seemed to be distributed at random, so that sometimes the answer to the question 'Does the patient have a history of violence?' was 'Yes' and sometimes 'No', often on successive days — the contradiction never once being remarked by those who supposedly cared for the patient. Nor, when the answer to the question was 'Yes' did anyone think to ask in what way or circumstances had the patient been violent.

After studying hundreds of pages of such documents it was impossible to form any impression of the patient or what, if anything, was wrong with him, or even why he was a patient at all. I remember the late Professor Michael Shepherd telling me that a series of books published annually, titled *Recent Progress in Psychiatry*, ought really to have been titled *Recent Activity in Psychiatry*, the editors not being able to distinguish between activity and progress. It seemed to me that a similar confusion obtained here between activity and work.

The problem was that the staff was stupid, or rather stupefied by the meaningless, dull, repetitious and time-consuming procedures that they were obliged to carry out. These obscured from them the real purpose of their work. Completing forms was not an aid to their work, but had become the work itself.

The nurses and others thought they were working merely because they were performing tasks laid down for them by their superiors. When they had filed a form they felt that sense of accomplishment that one experiences on completing a task. That the information contained on the form they had just filled was either useless or contradictory did not occur to or worry them. Perhaps this was because if they had noticed or worried about it, they would have despaired.

The staff had come — understandably — to believe that following procedure was an end in itself and had no connection with any other purpose. The responsibility for this lamentable state of affairs was that of the administration which was itself, no doubt, under pressure to conform to higher levels of procedure.

I was naïve enough not to realise that the main purpose of a report such as ours was to justify immobilism and to confirm that, apart from a slight mistake or two, all was for the best in this the best of all possible worlds. I did not have a say in the writing of the report and my conclusions were diluted down to the last homoeopathic strength, so that not one molecule of them remained in the solution. The prose of the report was impenetrable.

I went to see the Medical Director of the hospital in which the murders had been committed. He was affable enough in a distant way, the kind of bird whose feathers could not be ruffled. He sat imperturbably at his desk, ready to hear what I had to say and even readier to answer.

'The fundamental problem', I said, 'is that your staff don't know what they're doing.'

He did not leap to their defence; indeed, he nodded as if in agreement. I must admit I was impressed by his calm, considering that I was implicitly accusing him of being at the head of a useless and incompetent organisation. But he knew that already.

'They don't think about their work,' I said. 'They just fill in forms.'

He seemed to be in full accord with what I was saying. He was waiting for something that he did not know already.

'They fill in the forms in a mutually contradictory way,' I said.

I had finally goaded him into speech.

'That's the standard demanded these days,' he said.

'They don't even take a history.'

'Yes, I know,' he said. 'But we're supposed to demedicalise the service as much as possible.'

'I'm all in favour of demedicalisation,' I said. 'But you have to take a history to know whether a case is not medical.'

'I agree.'

'But you're the medical director,' I said.

'I don't agree with what's going on but there's nothing I can do about it.'

There was a finality to his words that made it quite pointless for me to say anything else. He was a large man physically, and he reminded me of one of the reclining Buddhas that I had seen on my travels in the east. He was nearing retirement and would draw a pension on which he could live comfortably for the rest of his life. If he had ever wanted to reform anything, or resist foolishness, that time was long past. I was left feeling like Bambi in a world of Panzer tanks.

My own hospital asked me once to produce an internal report on the treatment of a similar patient who had killed someone and then committed suicide. He had obviously been mad and so technically his homicide was not a murder. He had not been treated properly before he killed and one of the reasons was that, in the eighteen months prior to what is always called in these circumstances the 'index event', he had seen seventeen mental-health workers, only two of them twice. None of them, then, could have known him very well, let alone formed a trusting personal relationship with him.

It hardly takes much reflection to understand the inefficiency of this, to say nothing of its inhumanity.

A doctor who knows his patient well will often be able to tell how he's faring the moment he sees him, by his face, his bearing, his gait; but such implicit knowledge cannot be communicated in writing or by computer records, and is of course entirely lost when no one ever sees the patient more than twice. Wasteful as well as cruel, it has been the policy of successive governments to make medical practice as impersonal as possible, to the point of treating patients as the parcel in a game of pass-the-parcel. It is strange how, after the doubling of the number of doctors, it is more difficult than ever for patients to consult the same doctor twice.

Working in a system that seems always on the verge of a crisis, at the very maximum of its capacity, can have certain advantages, at least for those who take a pride in their work. One can derive satisfaction from having risen to do the seemingly impossible. But when the crisis becomes chronic, if that is not an oxymoron, it erodes moral and turns people into cynics and clock-watchers.

I remember a patient who arrived in our hospital who claimed to be at the centre of a world conspiracy in which 'they' (whoever 'they' were) were plotting to kill her and her three children. In order to avoid this fate both for herself and for them, she planned to kill the children and then herself.

There was nothing histrionic about her distress. If anything, it was underplayed. It was curious, of course, that she should have come to hospital rather than have gone, say, to the police. But the latter might well have been in league with them. Perhaps she came to the hospital because, at some level in her mind, she recognised that the alleged conspiracy was a manifestation of her own illness rather than a fact about the world. Or a hospital might have seemed to her the safest place in an unsafe world. At any rate, I thought that she meant what she said and would indeed kill her three children and herself if I let her go. I decided that she should be admitted as a matter of urgency to a psychiatric hospital.

Unfortunately, she was domiciled a hundred miles away. The hospital of her area said it had no beds and, in any case, she was no longer their responsibility because she was now physically in our area. But the hospital for our area claimed exactly the opposite — that she was not their responsibility because she was domiciled a hundred miles away.

No greater emergency could well be imagined. The patient had left her children with a friend and, if she left the hospital, would collect them and then likely kill them. Such killings, while not common, occur regularly. I had a patient who had gassed his three children in his car but was himself saved.

The woman had to be put under guard in case she tried to leave, which she did several times. I also could not leave until I found a place for her — a process that took nine hours of incessant telephone calls. No hospital within a radius of fifty or more miles would take her, all on the same grounds: no beds and no responsibility in the case. It was only by threatening my own hospital's administrators with an appeal to the Secretary of State for Health that I finally found a place for her. I left the hospital relieved and exhausted, angry rather than exhilarated by my eventual bureaucratic success. I had been both busy and bored. What I had achieved should have taken five minutes.

The constant reduction in the number of beds for psychiatric patients caused much waste of time, led to the double occupancy of beds (as soon as a patient was granted leave his bed was occupied by someone else, thus postponing the crisis until the first patient returned, leaving it for someone else to solve), and meant that only the most disturbed or dangerous patients could be admitted so that wards themselves became dangerous places whose residents agitated each other and violence was permanently in the air.

The reduction in the number of beds was the result of a coincidence of interests: the cost-cutters of the government on the one hand, and the ideologists of psychosis as the consequence of social injustice on the other, who denied that it was ever necessary to treat psychotics in hospital at all.

It so happened that some of the research on which the policy of constant reduction was conducted in my area. A psychiatrist, more ambitious I think to make a name than to cleave to the facts, had run the services in a catchment area, with the express purpose of hardly ever admitting any of his patients to hospital. He published the results of this experiment, which was influential in formulating the policy of the whole country. (If you want to influence people, tell them what they want to hear).

The author of the good news went on prolonged leave and I was asked to take over for a time. Shortly after I began I was asked to the house where a young lunatic was alarming his neighbours by his aggressive manner and loud and angry conversations with no visible interlocutors in the middle of the night. Before going to see him, I looked at the notes pertaining to him. He had been visited several times by the 'team', including by the psychiatrist who wanted to make a mark by reforming the world, or reform the world by making a mark. No one had hinted that he was dangerous.

I arrived at the small Victorian terraced house, better than anything of the kind that our own more enlightened and advanced age has been able to build. A middle-aged West-Indian man, the patient's next-door neighbour, was waiting outside his house for my arrival.

'You've got to do something, doc,' he said, 'or someone's going to be killed.'

He told me that the patient, in his twenties, had driven his terrified mother from the house, of which she was the owner, some months before. She had feared for her life and now lived elsewhere. The young man was menacing everyone around him, and it was obvious (said his neighbour) that he was mad and dangerous.

Foolhardily, no doubt, I knocked on his door.

Everyone at some point in his life likes to play the saviour of others, or of a Daniel come to judgment, and this was my moment. I would liberate the street from its fear. I would fearlessly confront the man and give him what Dr Willis, who treated George III, called 'the eye'.

I heard shouting that came from inside the house. The

neighbour had assured me that he was on his own and that no one else had been in the house for weeks. To my surprise, the door opened and there before me stood a young black man of fierce aspect, barefoot and with wild eyes. He was dishevelled and behind him I could see the remains of months lived as a madman — piles of clothes mixed with the rotting remains of half-eaten food, strewn papers and upturned furniture. I was not altogether disappointed when he slammed the door in my face.

Echoing General Macarthur to the neighbour, I vowed to return: this time with all the staff legally and practically necessary to take him against his wishes to hospital, including the police. And this I did.

It was only later that one of the nurses on the team told me something I had not known when I visited the young man for the first time.

'You know,' she said, 'that the last time the doctor visited him, the man came at him with a machete and he had to run away.'

Nothing of this appeared from the notes. The psychiatrist, in fact, had specifically forbidden any mention of the episode, or similar episodes in the cases of other patients, in the notes. He said that such records acted to the detriment of the patient's repute and created prejudice against him.

The psychiatrist also had race on the brain. For him racism was the single most important explanatory factor for the woes of the world. (Away from his favourite subject, he was a charming and amusing man with whom one could spend an enjoyable evening.) And it happens that a disproportionate number of young black men in Britain become psychotic, and are detained and treated against their will in hospital. So in addition to keeping all admissions to hospital down to zero, he thought he was fighting the good fight against institutional racism.

In this, I have little doubt that he thought he was acting the role of a latter-day William Wilberforce. For him the young man's madness was a response to the injustice he must have suffered, *ex officio* as a young black man, and to have treated him against his wishes would have been to compound the injustice. His madness, then, was not illness (or the result of smoking too much strong cannabis, say), but a reaction, even a reasonable one, to his experiences of life. If he went at people with machetes, it was only in self-defence.

But what of the neighbours, many of them also black? What of the mother, who had arrived in the country penniless, had worked for years to buy her house, and now found herself a refugee from her own son? They, presumably, were due no sympathy because they had gone over so entirely, and cravenly, to the white petty bourgeoisie. No doubt the mother was one of those contemptible women who dressed beautifully on Sundays, in spotless white gloves, broad-brimmed hat and impeccable frock, and went to church to speak in tongues, not understanding that she was partaking of the opium of the people.

I took the episode in good part, I think, not holding it deeply against the psychiatrist that he might have been indirectly responsible for my early demise or, worse still, my permanent disfigurement by a machete. (It was instructive that so many machetes and baseball bats were owned in the area. Cane was not cut there, nor was baseball ever played.

The ratio of sold baseball bats to baseballs might be a good measure of the violence of a society.) But I had my revenge on him, albeit in a peculiar and roundabout way.

One day I was telephoned by a local television company and asked whether I would take part in a discussion programme. As I had not watched television for many years, indeed for several decades, I thought that discussion programmes were still like The Brains' Trust of the 1950s, when viewers sent in questions such as 'Can there be drugs to make us happy?' and Dr Grey Walter, famous scientist of the time, would say to another panellist, Aldous Huxley, 'I think you're mistaken, Huxley, to imagine…' etc.

The discussion programme was a little different. I suppose I should have suspected as much from the subject of the discussion — exorcism.

This seemed to me an odd subject a quarter of a millennium after the Enlightenment and one of which I was ignorant, and in which, moreover, I was uninterested. I had tried to use ignorance of the subject as a reason why the television company should find someone else to appear. But ignorance is no disqualification in the modern world of media, and the young employee of the company insisted that I should nevertheless be perfect for the programme. Being weak, I gave way.

My idea of the programme was of four people at the most sitting round a table like a committee and talking among themselves, with a chairman whose only task was to ensure that one of them did not hog the limelight. It was not at all like that. There was a large audience of workers bussed in from a local factory that had been plied with drink. It was

seated in a kind of tribune erected in the studio. I subsequently learned that the main hope of the producers was that a
violent quarrel would break out, and even a resort to fists.
This was not an enquiry after truth but a gladiatorial spectacle
for the idle bored. And further to my surprise I was seated not
in the centre of the studio but in the midst of the tribune.

A bishop (of a church he had himself founded) gave his
view of the necessity of exorcism of those who had been
possessed by evil spirits and then the presenter of the show
— for it was by now obvious even to me that it was a show
rather than a discussion — asked a man seated next to me
what he thought of the exorcism he had undergone.

He was a former soldier who had fought in the Falklands,
had seen terrible things there and returned very disturbed,
drinking too much and violent when drunk (what he was like
before, no one enquired), in trouble with the police, and so
forth. Then he met two exorcists — American — who
exorcised him by making him vomit the evil spirit possessing
him into a bucket (there was a video of the process).
Apparently, the evil spirit took the material form of a little
creature, green in colour if my memory serves, but the video
did not capture it jumping ship, as it were.

Anyhow, the man was utterly changed after the exorcism.
He stopped drinking and instead of punching people in the
face, he helped old ladies across the road. In the language of
psychobabble, he had dealt with his demons. The presented
turned to me once this recitation was over and asked, 'As a
doctor, what do you think of that?'

I was in a false position. I was surrounded by a drunken
audience which almost certainly would have believed the man

and would have been in maudlin sympathy with him. If I started to dissect his story from a rational point of view, I am sure the audience would have turned against me and accused me of being a toff. The show was clearly intended to be a contest between the self-satisfied expert and the common man, to the great advantage of the latter.

In any case, it would have been wrong to disabuse the man of his illusions, which he appeared to be genuinely under, if they had resulted in a better life for him and everyone around him, all the more so when to have disillusioned him would also have been a public humiliation for him. I said something fatuously anodyne, more or less that I was glad that he felt better.

I fled the studio feeling a fool. Viewers might have had the impression that I did not disbelieve in exorcism and thought it more or less analogous to amputation of a gangrenous leg. It took me a few hours to console myself that, in this world of appearances, nothing is as transitory as an appearance on television. I resolved never to appear again. (A resolution I have not quite kept.)

A couple of weeks later, the television company, evidently impressed by my feeble performance, called me again and asked whether I could take part in another such programme, this time to discuss psychiatric patients who kill. I excused myself as having a previous engagement, but I said that I knew a man who would fit their bill exactly, namely the psychiatrist whose views might have resulted in my death — though I admit I merely volunteered to the television company that he was a psychiatrist. Although he and I did not agree on much, we were alike in never watching television, and he would almost certainly fall for the same patter as I had fallen for.

Like me he naively agreed to appear and this time the surprise was sprung the other way round. He was asked while sitting in the middle of the audience to give his opinion on the relationship between schizophrenia and murder. He gave a little academic talk about how there was no cause for panic, that the number and proportion of murders committed by schizophrenics had not increased, and that psychiatric patients were far more likely to be the victims of violence than perpetrators of it.

'Thank you, professor,' said the presenter, and then turned to the woman sitting next to him who had been widowed the week before when her husband had been murdered by a schizophrenic.

12

Psychiatric Fungus

Everyone Is a Patient

There are those who think that psychiatric patients should never, under any circumstances, be treated against their will. Among these was the late Thomas Szasz, an American psychiatrist of Hungarian origin who was a brilliant polemicist and prose stylist in his third language, English. Among his greatest achievements was the publication of an hilarious paper in the *Lancet*, not generally known (since the demise of its first editor, Thomas Wakley) for its light-heartedness or sense of humour. Szasz suggested in this paper that happiness be henceforth considered as a psychiatric condition because it was rare, often led to bad decisions and was rarely justified by objective conditions. It was therefore delusory.

He was drawing attention — correctly, in my view — to the tendency for psychiatric diagnosis to spread like fungus over the whole of human experience, emotion and conduct. Everyone is a patient and nothing is a manifestation just of itself.

Moreover, as Szasz pointed out, psychiatric conditions

were mainly unconnected with any discernible physical pathology (laboratory analysis), nor were any of their causes known. In other words (according to him) they were diseases only in a metaphorical sense. Really, they were just patterns of behaviour, often socially disagreeable or disadvantageous, but not diseases. To coerce people into treatment, so-called, for one of these patterns of behaviour was tyrannous in the extreme, not different in principle from the coercion employed by totalitarian regimes. In his opinion, then, when a madman committed a criminal act he should be punished exactly as if he had been sane: for he was not ill, he was merely bad. Treatment for such people was only medicalised policing and all the worse for its veil of philanthropy.

A mutual friend of Szasz' and mine, the development economist also of Hungarian origin, Peter Bauer, said that he had always wanted to hear us discuss this matter, and he invited us both to dinner one day when Szasz was in London. He was well into his seventies then, but still full of fire in defence of his ideas.

He was the kind of man, not very frequently encountered, who took disagreement in good part (admittedly by then he must have had a lot of experience of it), and had no animus towards those who disagreed with him.

I agreed with him to a considerable extent, that undesirable or undesired behaviour or emotion had been incontinently categorised as disease. But I could not agree with him that, until and unless such behaviour were proved to be the consequence of physical pathology, they must never be considered disease.

We are not yet in the position of intelligent Mr Toad, who,

like all those young men at Oxford, 'knows all there is to be knowed.' It is not plausible that behaviour previously ascribed to moral defect should actually be a disease once a physical cause has been discovered, whereas before it was not.

It might well be true that not to accept Szasz's clear dichotomy — either demonstrable pathology or no illness — might lead to a slippery slope, but if the slope actually existed in fact it could not be wished away simply because its existence makes it difficult for us to avoid abuses. The solution was to exercise judgment, not to deny reality.

And then I produced what was, in my own estimate, a decisive argument taken from real experience.

As it happened, I had been on duty for the prison the night before and I had been called to see a prisoner who had stripped himself naked and was trying to connect himself to the light socket. He talked gibberish that no one could understand and he was in a world into which nothing we said could obtrude. He had also tried to eat the lightbulb.

His madness had come on very suddenly, he had no previous record of it, and he had behaved perfectly normally until that very evening. In all likelihood he had taken some drug or other. I had once learned to ask the way in Turkish — but not to understand the answer. It was the same here: I could ask but I could not understand the answer.

And since the prisoner was behaving in a way hazardous to himself, I ordered that he be sedated, which entailed that the officers held him down by force while I injected him with the tranquilliser.

The officers were increasingly nervous about doing such a thing in case they were accused of assault, but I assured them that as it was I who gave the order, it was I who would take the blame. And they trusted me not to 'slope shoulders', as the process of shifting blame on to someone else was called.

The next morning the man had recovered fully. This confirmed that the most likely diagnosis was an acute psychotic reaction to something he had taken. But we could never know for certain, tests being out of the question and in any case potentially inconclusive.

What would he have done in this situation, I asked Szasz?

He said the he would not have been in the situation in the first place, which was that of assisting the state in its work of repression of crime.

That, it seemed to me, was a complete evasion. Szasz acknowledged the rightness of the principle of punishment, indeed it was a cornerstone of his philosophy that the illegal behaviour of lunatics should be dealt with in precisely the same way as any other illegal behaviour. Lunacy was only illness metaphorically-speaking, and in effect lunatics were merely constructing excuses for themselves that some were gullible enough to believe.

There was nonetheless something in this, as in so much of what Szasz said. It was by no means unknown for a psychiatric patient to say to an arresting policeman, 'You can't touch me, I'm a schizophrenic.' But again, also as in so much of what Szasz said, a partial truth was taken for the whole.

I admired Szasz. Things had not been easy for him. It had been difficult for him when he arrived in America to gain admission to medical school because many schools operated a *numerus clausus* against Jews. But this only fired Szasz' determination. Prejudice, provided it is neither universal nor legally enforced, is not an insuperable barrier to social advance or other forms of success, and may actually be a spur to it.

In the final analysis, I came away from my dinner with Szasz that he was a man who had fallen in love with his own ideas, original and insightful as they had been, and turned them into a key to answer all questions, even to the practical extent of denying prisoners medical attention.

Such men as he are necessary but also dangerous, notwithstanding their admirable affability. It was a good principle to be wary of treating people against their will, or of ascribing their actions to madness over which they had no control — that way tyranny lies. But the opposite extreme has also to be guarded against.

There was once a prisoner who was on remand for murder and who conversed regularly with the television in his cell, whether it was on or off. (Television is the modern 'liquid cosh'. It is used to keep the prisoners quiet, or at least occupied.) His conversations with the television were mainly angry, as if he were an exceptionally stern critic of what was, or had been, shown on it. It was impossible to distract him from his angry expostulations and, like other patients in such a condition, he was clearly in a world of his own. No sense could be made of what he said.

He was a large, powerful and very nasty man with a long history of serious violence to others, but he also had a history of madness exacerbated by a tendency to take drugs known to cause or exacerbate madness. His violence preceded his madness, of which it might have been a prodrome or a manifestation of his underlying character. His manner was extremely menacing, and I made him 'three to unlock', that is to say that his cell door was not to be opened unless there were at least three officers present.

I both telephoned and wrote to his lawyer to inform him that, in my opinion, his client was not only unfit to plead, but unfit to attend court, and needed admission to hospital. Whether he would ever be fit to plead or attend court I could not say.

The lawyer, with perfect reason, asked the psychiatrist who had treated him in the past for his opinion. This psychiatrist, who was a mild-mannered and thoroughly decent man, came to the prison and prepared a report that astonished me.

In it he said that the man was normal and that his habit of talking angrily to the television was in keeping with his cultural background, which was (in a previous generation) Jamaican. This was the first time I had ever heard it said that Jamaicans talked to their televisions.

With perfect reason, his lawyer preferred my colleague's report to mine. After all, his knowledge of the man was greater and of much longer-standing than was mine. I had never met the man before his present incarceration. And so, on the appointed day, the man — with difficulty — was hauled off to court for the beginning of his trial.

Fortunately the dock these days, the place in court where the accused stands or sits, is rarely the little box open to the rest of the court, but a space at the rear of the court, separated from it by a thick pane of bullet-proof glass, large enough to hold several accused persons at once (and their gaolers) in cases of joint enterprise. The proceedings of the court, and the words of the accused, other than any formal testimony in his own defence that he might give, are relayed to each other by microphones that can be switched off. No doubt these new-style docks are themselves implicit testimony to the increased violence of our society, but in this case they proved their worth. In America, whose trials are in some respects inferior to our own, the accused sits next to his lawyer like a normal person, which makes communication with him easier and more supple. The difference is evidence of what many people are reluctant to believe, namely that our society is now more violent than it is in most of America.

The sight of armed policemen bearing semi-automatic weapons has certainly become ever more frequent, if my career is a witness. I never found this sight particularly reassuring as far as my own safety was concerned. One mad policeman with a semi-automatic could do a lot of murder in a courthouse in which hundreds of people mill. I once arrived at the intensive care unit of my hospital to find policemen similarly armed sitting at the end of two beds opposite each other, the occupants of which belonged to two enemy gangs. They had shot each other at the same time, seriously wounding but not killing each other. To quote Hamlet, that it should come to this! It was a scene unthinkable at the outset of my career.

Once he had been manoeuvred into the dock, the accused in this case took no interest in the proceedings, but paced up and down menacingly like a caged tiger, muttering constantly to himself. On the second day of the trial, a Friday, the judge halted it and asked both my colleague and I to attend court, most unusually, on the following Saturday morning. It was the only time I ever gave evidence in court with the judge not wearing his paraphernalia.

My evidence was straightforward. The man was mad, he was unfit to plead, he was unfit to attend court, and he might not recover even if treated. He ought to be admitted to hospital.

My colleague then gave his evidence. I found it a painful experience to listen to him. At first, he defended his thesis that the man's behaviour was normal for one of his cultural background. Little by little, however, in the face of the judge's incredulity, he was forced to concede that it was perhaps a little unusual and more in keeping with his previous psychotic state than with normality. Finally, after further twisting and turning, he agreed that it would be best if the man were admitted to hospital.

I think it was obvious to everyone in the court that his initial diagnosis of normality was inspired by fear.

I had suspected from the outset that my colleague was what is called, in a mealy-mouthed way, culturally sensitive, and that cultural sensitivity was being used as an excuse not to have to treat a man who was both difficult and dangerous. He was the kind of man who could smash up a room in no time, and was nobody's idea of the perfect guest. Indeed, he struck terror in my heart. He was also the kind of madman with the strength of ten. But that did not alter the fact that he needed treatment (which might not work) and was not fit to stand trial.

On his last admission to hospital the man had seriously injured two nurses, and understandably they did not want him back. The hospital did not prosecute him, on the general grounds that, 'We don't prosecute our patients.' Had the hospital done so, he would have been confined to an institution of maximum security.

In a matter of less than half an hour, the psychiatrist's patient had gone from having nothing wrong with him to being so dangerous as a consequence of his madness that he required treatment in conditions of far greater security than his psychiatrist could offer. This, no doubt, was what had been in the judge's mind in the first place when he called us into court, but it was acutely uncomfortable to watch the exposure of my colleague's cowardice.

Not that I was not once myself guilty of similar such cowardice. A black man in his twenties had been admitted to our hospital having cut his wrists. These were not the delicate cuts of the deliberate self-harmer (another innovation of our era), but slashes of Senecan proportion and depth. It is a mistake to judge the seriousness of suicidal intent by the seriousness or otherwise of that attempt — people can die without meaning to do so, as they can (more often) survive without meaning to do so.

In this case, however, there was no mistaking the seriousness of the attempt. He had not been known to make trivial gestures, had slashed his wrists to such an extent that they required surgical repair and had lost so much blood that he had to be transfused, and, above all, he had barricaded his house so that no one should find him. It required the police to break in when his mother suspected that something was wrong.

He was virtually mute as he lay in his hospital bed. His mother, at first an amiable and sensible woman, gave an unequivocal history of change in his in his mood, character and conduct over the previous six weeks or so. Before that he had been a steady, hard-working young man of normal and unexceptional enjoyments such as playing football and going out with his friends. Gradually, though, he had become morose and uncommunicative, had isolated himself from others, and had lost weight by not eating properly. His mother was unable to account for this change by anything that she knew of his life.

I could come to no diagnosis straight away, the possibilities were legion. But it was obvious from what she had said that he should be detained in hospital for further observation after he was physically fit to leave. At first his mother was in perfect agreement with my suggestion.

Alas, a friend of the young man, who claimed to be the person closest to him, turned up at the hospital. When he heard from the mother that I proposed to detain the patient in hospital he grew at once agitated and furiously angry, dancing around and jabbing the air with his finger, as though he were accusing the atmosphere of something.

'It's only because he's black that you want to keep him!' he said. 'Only because he's black. You're a racist!'

I tried to reason with him, appearing much calmer than I felt inside.

I explained that I was doing for him only what I would do for any other patient in a similar situation, that it was obvious that there was something very wrong with him, and that he desperately needed diagnosis and possibly treatment. But in this case, contrary to what it asserts in the Bible, a soft answer did not turn away wrath, but only increased it.

'He's a racist,' he said to the mother. 'He's only saying he should stay in hospital because he's black. If he was white, he wouldn't want to keep him in hospital.'

This was uttered with so much force and conviction, as being so self-evidently true, and moreover with so much anger, that his mother dared not contradict him, and from having been perfectly reasonable went herself over to belligerence, as if to appease him. I thought she was afraid of him.

I tried to draw her apart, to speak to her on her own, but he would not let me, interposing himself physically between us in a menacing manner.

What could I do? Although aggressive, he had done nothing to put him outside the law and I could not have asked for him to be removed from the premises. I was certain that had I attempted to do so she would have taken his part. After all, she would meet me at most two or three times more, and only briefly, but him she would meet constantly and he was in a position to make her life a hell. By his manner I thought he was probably more than willing to do so. Still I insisted for a time, but the patient's friend became more and more agitated, as did now his mother. He spoke of bringing other friends to the hospital to free the patient.

I foresaw a violent melee on the ward for the provocation of which I would be blamed. Only the person in authority in the modern world is held to be a moral agent, not the ordinary person.

I should have stuck to my guns, but I didn't.

'All right, then,' I said. 'I'll release him home, but on certain conditions.'

The conditions were that he was never left on his own, that doctors and nurses were allowed to visit him regularly, that they gave him any medication as directed, and that they signed a paper acknowledging not only all these conditions, but that I had strongly advised against his discharge from hospital because he was at serious risk of suicide — and that they had accused me of being a racist in suggesting that he should remain.

This they willingly, and in the case of the friend contemptuously, signed. They took the patient home, screwing up the piece of paper on which they had signed the agreement and throwing it on the ground immediately outside the ward, where I found it. About four weeks later I heard that he had killed himself with car exhaust. They had not kept to the conditions, of course; doctors and nurses had not been granted admission and they had not tried to force the issue.

Some time later I received a letter from the coroner asking me provide a report. This I did, not without a discreditable element of *Schadenfreude*, the tragedy of the young man's death notwithstanding. I had been insulted and been proved right.

Strictly speaking I could have overruled the mother and the friend (who had no legal standing in the affair) and there was a provision in the law for doing so. I could have been accounted negligent for not having invoked it. But I sent the coroner a copy of the conditions that they had signed, including their acknowledgement of having insulted me.

The mother's grief was no doubt worthy of compassion, but not at my expense for failure. I had been weak in putting the avoidance of a riot higher than the interest of my patient, but she had been similarly weak, and insulting to boot, and I could not find it in my heart to feel much guilt.

As for the 'friend', I don't suppose that he felt much regret, let alone guilt. I judged that he was capable of seamlessly incorporating every happenstance, every misfortune, into his paranoid view of the world, a view that gave him an armour-plated superiority to that world. It made a victim of him however he behaved; it freed him from the need for self-examination.

His error was not that he had a prejudice (in this case that racism explained all that happened in society). For all of us have, and cannot be without, prejudices when we go out into the world. Anyone who thinks he is without prejudice is fooling himself.

The young man's error was rather his unwillingness to examine his prejudice in the light of an individual case, an unwillingness that led, in this instance, to a disastrous end. But a world outlook is so precious to a man, as well as so fragile that it is endangered by a single counter-example, that he is willing to sacrifice life itself on its altar.

13

No Good Act...

I was sued for negligence only once, by a man who subsequently murdered his mother. I do not claim that the two events were connected in any way. But the case taught me a lesson all the same.

The man in question had been treated (not by me) for psychosis in the course of which he had been violent to others, including his mother. He was treated with powerful tranquillising drugs that sometimes, though rarely, have life-threatening side-effects. These his doctors failed to recognise in him until it was almost too late. He spent several weeks on the intensive care unit, where he survived but could easily have died.

Once he left hospital I heard no more from him for several years. Then, out of the blue, I received a letter from a solicitor who acted for him, asking for a medical report.

The man had decided to sue his doctors for negligence, but he had exceeded the time limit for bringing an action, unless he had a good and sufficient reason for the delay. Would I be prepared to write a report on whether there had been such a reason? I would not be paid unless there were such a reason accepted by the court. The man himself had no funds, and feeling the great philanthropist, I agreed to write a report for nothing. I read the man's medical records, which were very long, and prepared a report accordingly.

The law is that a man who believes himself to have been wronged must generally start proceedings within three years of what is called 'constructive knowledge' of the wrong done him. Constructive knowledge is knowledge the man may reasonably have been expected to possess in his circumstances. Delay in proceedings may be because the wrong done him may not be evident straight away; or a person may not be in a condition to start proceedings even if he has constructive knowledge, for example if he is paralysed. In this case, the plaintiff was for a long time insane after the wrong done him, which explained his delay. I wrote a report favourable to his case (that is to say, that there was a good reason for the delay in bringing his case, which eventually was settled out of court).

Again I heard no more from him for two or three years. Then, through the post, I received a scrappily-filled form indicating that he was claiming £250,000 in damages from me because he thought that my report omitted something that he thought it ought to have included, but which would have made no difference to the outcome of the case.

I was inclined to disregard this nonsense, to assign it to the waste-paper basket, but just before doing so I thought better of it and sent it to my medical defence organisation. It was as well that I did, for a lawyer told me that had I not answered his allegation, the claim would have gone by default and I would have been liable. My defence organisation's lawyer applied to the court to have the cases summarily dismissed as vexatious and was successful.

I had not been the only object of his attempts at litigation. He tried to sue almost everyone with whom he had come in professional or other contact. Before long he was prohibited from bringing any legal actions because he appeared to suffer from *paranoia querulans*, a form of persecution complex in which, as the name suggests, a querulent person constantly seeks redress for insignificant or non-existent wrongs that he thinks have been done him. The case taught me not to prepare reports *pro bono*, for, as the Hindi saying puts it, 'Why do you hate me when I've never tried to do anything for you?'

Although I was satisfied with the comparatively swift outcome of my case, I came to see our system of tort — compensation for wrongs done by one person or legal personality to another — as cumbersome and corrupting, if not actually corrupt. A case in which I was a witness distilled for me all the failings of the system.

A man had been exposed inadvertently to some noxious gas in the course of his work. It was very little and, at first, he noticed no ill-effects. But once it was discovered that a badly-maintained pipe had leaked the gas, he looked up the ill-effects on the internet and promptly began to suffer them. This was not mere surmise. It was conclusively proved in court to have been so.

Among the man's many symptoms — he became almost a textbook case, having in effect read a textbook — were severe headaches, continual fatigue, memory impairment, depression of mood and an inability to concentrate. He claimed that, by unhappy coincidence, his career had just been about to take off when he was exposed to the gas and that therefore his monetary loss was very great. In fact, there was no evidence of an incipient qualitative leap in his career before the exposure. Nevertheless, this speculation was made the basis of a claim for a sum of money that the plaintiff could never have accumulated in any other way than a winning lottery ticket. That this preposterous nonsense was entertained even for an instant was no credit to our legal system; and, win or lose, it would cost the man's employer a great deal of money.

The man had found expert neuropsychologists according to whose tests his inability to concentrate, etc., were caused by organic brain damage caused by exposure to the gas. The damage, they said, was permanent and irreversible. He would never be able to work again, not even in the menial capacity in which, in fact, he had been employed before.

My evidence was that this was all untrue. The man had showed abundant evidence of ability to concentrate since the exposure and, despite his claims of debilitating fatigue, had managed to go on a safari holiday in East Africa and another to the pyramids in Egypt. In other words, without actually saying so, I was accusing him of being a fraud.

The plaintiff took the stand and gave evidence in his own behalf. He was in the box for nearly two days, most of it under ferocious cross-examination by defence counsel, a young man who would clearly become one day soon a leader of his profession. The papers in the case, which had so far lasted three years, were by this time several thousand pages long. Counsel's command of them was very impressive. At a moment's notice he could refer to what in effect was page

3,119 of the papers, and go straight to it.

More to the point, however, the plaintiff and now witness himself had also mastered the papers in an impressive way, all since the accident that had supposedly deprived him totally of power of concentration. The only times he faltered were when he was asked questions that were clearly awkward for him to answer truthfully. Then he fell back on amnesia caused by brain damage.

I had said to the barrister during an adjournment, after it had been shown conclusively that he had suffered no symptoms until he had looked up the effects of exposure on the internet, 'We're home and dry!' (I confess that had felt from the start a strong desire that justice should be done and the plaintiff receive nothing, though of course as an expert I was on no one's side.) Naïve!

'Not at all,' said the barrister gloomily. 'It's very bad for us.'

How could that be? I could scarcely believe it, for it had demonstrated that the gas itself did him no harm.

'How so?' I asked.

'It will be held that if he had not been exposed to the gas in the first place, he would not have looked up its effects on the internet, and therefore that what he suffers is as much an effect of his exposure as if it had been the direct result of it.'

'But that's an open invitation to fraud,' I said.

'It's the law,' he said, pushing his wig on to the back of his head (as many barristers do when they are exasperated).

In the end the judge awarded the man about five per cent of what he had claimed.

It seemed to me an outrage that he should have been awarded anything at all, and the award of anything stood as a clear encouragement of lying and exaggeration. The employer was left with an enormous bill, for costs were awarded against him. Not only did he have to pay his own legal costs, including my fee of course (a comparative flea-bite), but the plaintiff's. The total must have been many hundreds of thousands of pounds.

In his judgment, the judge accepted the evidence of the neuropsychologists rather than that of his own eyes and ears: namely that the plaintiff, far from suffering any defect of concentration, was well above average in this respect, and certainly not deficient.

Of course, if the law as already laid down is that catching symptoms from the internet is to be equated with symptoms directly caused by a physical insult, he had no choice but to accept it. Finally, the judge appeared to conclude nothing about the plaintiff from the fact that he claimed twenty times more than he thought the claim was worth, a disparity surely too great to conclude anything but that the plaintiff was a liar and a gold-digger, as well as a perjurer who, far from being rewarded, ought to have been prosecuted and imprisoned.

I have been involved in cases in which plaintiffs have been awarded millions against hospitals and doctors who acted negligently and caused great harm, to some extent reparable by the award of money. But even here it is the taxpayer rather than the wrongdoer who is penalised. No doubt this is all for the best. Everyone makes mistakes and probably nearly everyone is negligent at some time or another (but most get away with it).

Life would be impossible for doctors if they were under threat of losing everything they had each time they acted.

They have therefore to be allowed to insure themselves, and share the risks with all their colleagues. But insurance is not justice and I have never known a case in which the person responsible for a costly error was much the loser by it. Often, negligence is not the fault of one person alone, but of a concatenation of small deficiencies, none of them a hanging offence. Responsibility is diffused, not least among those who might be expected to do the reprimanding.

Still, I did not think it a good idea for the directors of my hospital to let a firm of lawyers advertise on the screens provided to entertain the out-patients while they waited for their appointments. The firm or its agency had devised an inspiring little jingle:

Remember, where there's blame
There's a claim.

Could it be that some patients went into their consultation with the doctor hoping for some kind of negligence, serious enough to be worth some money but not serious enough to ruin their lives?

Humanity is sufficiently diverse for this to have been possible.

14

Loud Pleasures

I used to appear in the courts quite often. A trial is an organisational feat: to get judge, barristers and witnesses together is no easy task and I do not envy those who have to perform it. Since trials are not scripted, it is impossible to predict to the minute when a witness will 'get on', as the phrase for appearance in the witness box goes. There is sometimes a great deal of hanging about outside the court until one is called. Personally I did not mind this. Often I used to write an article or review a book while waiting. In addition, I would eavesdrop on the conversations of the accused on bail with the lawyers just before they went into court, which would give me material for another article; and finally I was also paid for my time as I waited.

In one case, however, even I grew a little tired of waiting. I had been told for three days that I would be called any time now. On the fourth day I complained to the counsel as a witness for whose side I was appearing.

'When am I going to get on?' I asked him, no doubt in a slightly aggrieved tone.

'What are you worried about?' counsel replied, so urbanely that I at once felt my naivety. 'The meter's still ticking, isn't it?'

I couldn't help laughing, of course. But still I felt a little disturbed by being compared with a taxi waiting outside the building for a fare to emerge. I could not altogether rid myself of the idea that this cavalier attitude to public expenditure would bring us eventually to rack and ruin even if, in the meantime, it benefited me to a minor extent.

The great French economic journalist of the nineteenth century, Frédéric Bastiat (the only writer on economics that makes you laugh) said that the state was the means by which everyone seeks to live at everyone else's expense. Whatever the literal truth or otherwise of this statement, I saw plenty of looting of the public pure, all of it perfectly legal as far as I could tell.

Once in the prison there was a prisoner from Angola, accused of a violent offence, who was obviously so mad that he was unfit to plead. He was what the officers called 'very verbal,' quite different from being 'mouthy' ('moufy') or 'lippy.' The latter two connoted willful insolence, and therefore were inexcusable; the former, madness, and therefore excusable. On the whole, the officers were fine connoisseurs of the difference.

I telephoned his lawyer to tell him that his client was mad and unfit to plead, or even to appear in court. He asked me whether I would write him a report to that effect and how much I would charge. I said that, as I already knew the man well and it involved practically no work, I would do it for nothing.

He said that on no account should I do that. It would set a very bad precedent, and drive down the costs of defending a client, which would be disastrous and contrary to legal principles. I then named a modest sum that nevertheless seemed generous enough to me — a very good restaurant meal for two, in return for five minutes' work — and he agreed.

A short time afterwards I received a call from the lawyer asking me to desist from writing my report. In the meantime, he said, he had found someone else to do it — at nearly nine times the cost. Admittedly, this person would have to come from an hour away, but coming to the conclusion that the prisoner was unfit to lead or stand trial would take no longer than five minutes. The fee was outrageous: it would have taken two skilled workers a couple of weeks of work at least to raise sufficient tax to pay it. The lawyer, I surmised, wanted an inflated bill from the psychiatrist to make his own look the more reasonable.

It was my custom to volunteer for duty over the Christmas period. I pretended it was a sacrifice, a manifestation of painful devotion, but in fact it was the perfect pretext not to participate in its enforced jollity that so depresses me. Hell for me is not other people, but other people having what they call a good time. In England, at least, jollity has an hysterical quality to it, as if there can be no enjoyment without the noisy demonstration that one is enjoying oneself — the noisiest person enjoying himself most. The English were a nation that took its pleasures sadly; now they are a nation that takes its pleasures loudly. It would be much better for them to suffer their pleasures in silence.

I liked Christmas in prison. There was a big Christmas tree in its Victorian panopticon heart, with a few mournful decorations hanging from the magnificent ironwork. There was no exchange of presents, of course, but there was a large Christmas lunch after which the prisoners slept like babies, except for the snores. I went round the hospital wing to wish the patients — mad, mostly, or at least psychologically disturbed — Merry Christmas. I took them chocolates, which they received with the gratitude of a murderer being sentenced to death.

I volunteered as usual to be on duty the last Christmas before I retired, initially an offer that was gratefully accepted.

But by then an administrator, brought in from outside, a specialist in the new queen of the sciences, management, was brought in, one suspects at a higher salary, to run the hospital.

A straw in the wind of increasing administrativeness had been the way in which the new hospital wing had been fitted out. The only room or office in it not to have a telephone was that of the doctor, whose calls, one might have supposed, were the most intimately connected to the ostensible purpose of the whole place. Ever afterwards, whenever I needed to talk to make a call about or on behalf of my patients, I had to find an available telephone somewhere else, in aggregate spending many hours doing so.

The administrator was the kind of man, increasingly common in the public service, who could not look you in the eye as you passed him in the corridor. There was something furtive about him, as though he were always aware at some level in his mind, that he was a superfluous if well-paid man — his job did not really exist except as an employment scheme that had been created for administrators like him in order that he should be paid a salary. Those responsible for such schemes could then think they had solved a problem, whatever it was, as they had spent (someone else's) money on it.

I suppose, in retrospect, that I should have felt sorry for him, for his was a miserable condition of bad faith in which to live. But at the time I didn't. It is wrong to think of men in zoological metaphors, but I thought of him as a result as a hybrid of a worm and a weasel.

Anyhow, three days before the Christmas in question, he (who never walked but he sidled) came to me to tell me that my services would not be required over Christmas after all, that he had made alternative arrangements for the next ten days.

The arrangements he had made were extraordinary from any rational point of view. He had found a British doctor working in Germany who would be flown over, put up in a five-star hotel, all meals included, and paid at a rate at least four times mine (which was admittedly so low that I never revealed it to colleagues). He had never worked in a prison before and apparently had been told that there would be almost nothing to do beyond the occasional distribution of an aspirin.

The flown-in doctor soon found out that this was not so. He was called to medical, surgical and psychiatric emergencies on his first day, including a man who had tried to hang himself. He resigned and demanded to be flown back to Germany. He had been misled about the work and did not feel safe doing it.

On Christmas Day, therefore, I received a somewhat sheepish phone call from the duty governor, a woman of intelligence, good humour and good sense, whom I much respected, who asked me whether I would do the prison a favour and agree to go back on duty as previously arranged.

As is so often the case, the person responsible for making the mess was not the one who had to clear it up. I was in a position of strength. It was a legal requirement — quite correctly so — that the prison should have medical cover at all times. I could have complained about the administrator and demanded triple pay, but I just agreed, without conditions, to the request.

I had no desire to make the duty governor squirm or beg, and instead indulged myself in the delightful sin of pride, that is to say in my own decency and public spirit. I took up the baton dropped by the other doctor — whom, incidentally, I never met, the administrator considering that no kind of handover was necessary — without fuss.

I did try, however, and have tried ever since, to think of the hospital administrator's reasons for making his strange arrangement.

It certainly could not have been the need for economy. Nor could it have been the betterment of the service, for not even he could have supposed that the employment of an untried person in a position of which he had no experience in place of someone of at least adequate competence could have represented a betterment of the service. There was not one other explanation that I could think of other than an instinctive dislike of me (perhaps modern managers have highly-developed antennae for those who are underwhelmed). But even that reason I rejected: who would pay £15,000 for something meaningless, involving an unsuspecting third party? There must have been an administrative reason, but it remains fathomless to me to this day. Within three months he was promoted to a higher level in penal administration, with several prisons now falling under his remit.

Frédéric Bastiat would have liked another instance of modern management.

A young man was sent to me for examination by an insurance company. Shortly before, he had taken out insurance against chronic illness whose premiums — he being a fit and healthy young man — were very modest. Here it is perhaps worth mentioning that the only two murderers I met who had killed for insurance money had induced their victims to increase the amount insured shortly before by ten times. They did not wait for many premiums, which had increased proportionately, of course, before striking. This would have given a clue even to Dr Watson.

Lo and behold, soon after taking out his insurance, the fit and healthy young man was struck down with a condition known as chronic fatigue syndrome. This is not the place to rehearse the cause of the syndrome, or pattern of behaviour, which some think is a chronic consequence of an occult viral infection and others a modern form of what in the nineteenth century was called neurasthenia.

At any rate, it is characterised by extreme fatigue on the slightest exertion and can last for many years, up to a whole lifetime. There are no laboratory tests for the condition. Indeed, finding a physical cause for the fatigue precludes the diagnosis, which can be made only after it has lasted several months and when there is no accepted medical explanation for it.

The insurance company with which the young man had

insured himself recognised chronic fatigue syndrome as an illness like any other. Whether it ought to have done so — whether, indeed, it had any choice in the matter — is beside the point. It did, and it sent me the young man to determine whether he fulfilled the criteria for making the diagnosis.

This was a matter of a checklist: if enough boxes were ticked, he had the condition and was entitled to an income from the company, perhaps for the rest of his life, which might have been for sixty years or more.

The young man arrived in the hospital in T-shirt and shorts. I had read his medical notes and noted that three years before he had made a similar claim from another insurance company, which been turned down, for chronic back pain, a condition that is difficult to disprove and which correlates ill with physical pathology. But the fact that he had made a claim deemed inadmissible before did not mean that his current claim was fraudulent. After all, even the worst hypochondriac falls ill and dies — otherwise, hypochondriasis would be the elixir of life.

The young man must have researched his supposed condition on the internet, for he gave a perfect history of it. He had prepared his ground well and in a certain sense diligently. He had gone to his doctor many times over the previous months complaining of extreme fatigue made instantaneously worse by any kind of effort, including mental, and claimed to have spent most of his time in bed, unable to do anything but rest.

He had girded up his loins to come to me, but with such difficulty, he said, that he had seriously considered cancellation. I could find no reason for denying the diagnosis, other than my fundamental disbelief in its *bona fides*, and told the insurance company so: though I telephoned its chief doctor to tell him that I suspected fraud.

I thought no more of the case until about three months later, when I received a video film through the post from the insurance company with a letter asking me whether what the video showed was compatible with what the young man had told me.

The video showed him — since my examination of him — climbing ladders and scaffolding to paint or re-roof houses. Clearly this was not compatible with the claim that the slightest exertion exhausted him. I wrote to the company to this effect.

I also spoke to the company's doctor again.

'I trust you're going to prosecute him for fraud,' I said.

'No,' he said. 'We never do that.'

'Why not?' I asked.

'Our customers wouldn't like it.'

'Your honest ones would.'

'Well, we don't do it.'

Individual cases of fraud hardly mattered to the company. They merely passed on the costs to their customers, plus a commission no doubt. The only limitation on the scale of fraud was imposed by the existence of other insurance companies, with competing premium rates. Within this cartelised constraint, only a certain degree of vigilance against fraud was required, not an attempt at suppression or even deterrence.

The matter did not end quite there. The young man by now knew his insurance companies well.

He knew that he would not be prosecuted, but that was not all. He knew that the trade association of insurers had a rule according to which a claimant could appeal if he were turned down, and in the meantime the company would have to pay the income he would have received had his claim been accepted, until such time as the complaint was resolved. This money was irrecoverable by the company even if the complaint were not upheld.

The young man complained about my report. Not about its contents which, superficially, were favourable to his case, but because I had kept him waiting for fifteen minutes in the corridor outside my room. This complaint was, of course, entirely frivolous and vexatious, but the young man was shrewd. He knew that the insurance company was as vast a bureaucracy as a government department and that its wheels ground very slowly. It would therefore take several months before his complaint was resolved, several months during which he would be paid as if his claim had been accepted. In a way, it was an admirable display of Machiavellianism on a petty scale.

Could his reward have been worth the scheming?

I suspect that in cases such as this one, much of the reward is non-monetary. It was the feeling of having triumphed over the world that mattered, and, had he been able to make ten times the amount of money by the same expenditure of effort and ingenuity, but by honest means, he would have rejected the opportunity. There is a pleasure in being rewarded where one deserves punishment.

It is curious that those who are awarded large sums in compensation are seldom followed-up to see whether their injuries remit as a result. The human mind is a somewhat complex instrument, in which fraud can easily turn to true belief (and *vice versa*, and everything in between). Thus the injury will endure, even if its origin is purely psychological; for if it does not endure, the person will stand revealed to himself as a fraud.

Even in an age of dishonesty most people do not like to think of themselves as such. The great prophet, Falstaff, said 'I will turn diseases to commodity,' but he was a man with exceptional self-knowledge. Most people who claim navigate between fraud and true belief, without quite reaching the shores of either.

The new legal doctrine that psychological injury and disorder is to be treated in precisely the same way as physical injury is, of course, another incitement to fraud, to the great benefit of the legal and psychiatric professions. It is true that the mental and the physical cannot be altogether disentangled, that an injury that will lay one man low will be shrugged off as trivial by another. But the fact that the disentanglement cannot be perfect does not mean that no effort should be made.

There is no reason to treat whiplash injury (a condition that, in its chronic form, exists only where compensation for it is possible and almost automatic) and tetraplegia as in principle the same — indeed, it is rather insulting to tetraplegics to do so — even though everyone knows that the great majority of whiplash symptoms, where they are not faked, are of psychological origin.

Judges seem often to be blinded by, and express credulity towards, psychological tests. They sometimes regard them with the reverence afforded the Golden Calf. Graphs and talk of standard deviations dazzle them.

I remember the case of a man of seventy who was accused of a sexual crime committed fifty years earlier (there is now no statute of limitations on such crimes, no doubt because of media hysteria). The defence alleged that the man was unfit for trial and produced psychological reports to demonstrate that he was incapable of doing what in fact he did every day.

I argued, unsuccessfully, that whatever happens must be possible. He lived a normal, if restricted, life, shopping, budgeting, going on outings and so forth. He knew what he was charged with and had instructed his lawyers with perfect coherence. Nevertheless, the judge chose to prefer the graphs and statistics demonstrating that he could do none of these things. Of this, though I thought it a very doubtful or even dishonest finding, I was rather glad.

The doctrine that the psychological or mental is not to be distinguished from the physical is probably founded on a crude and reductionist materialism (materialism in the philosophical rather than the economic sense, though here they may to an extent coincide). No one can live or experience life as if this philosophy were true in his own case, though he might use it to claim advantages — exculpation, for example — on occasion. The doctrine is a disaster for everyone and a cause itself of much disability and misery, though only in so far as there are rewards for believing it.

15

A Simple Caution

Perhaps I make it appear that I detest lawyers and regard them all as crooks, but this is very far from the case. I often liked and admired them, from the modest solicitor who attended a police station in the middle of the night to advise a small-time drunken malefactor on how to respond, if at all, to police questioning, to the grand, famous and brilliant Queen's Counsel who can make white black and black white, all with the utmost intellectual elegance and personal charm or courtesy.

The caution given to arrested persons before the police questioned them changed in my time, in my opinion for the worse. Originally the caution was very simple, that the suspect did not have to say anything, but if he did say something it would be taken down and could be used in evidence against him. It was changed to something more complex. The suspect is still told that he does not have to say anything, but if he refuses to tell the police something that he subsequently relies on in court and that he could have told them, the court might draw an inference from his refusal.

I discussed this with a friend who is a High Court judge. He thought the change — the semi-abrogation of the right not to incriminate yourself — unimportant because in practice no court *did* draw any conclusions from a suspect's silence during police questioning. He thought, however, that the new caution might speed the administration of justice.

I did not agree. First, the new caution had an unmistakable undertone of menace about it absent from the old. There is no better way to obtain a false confession from someone than to frighten him with harmful consequences if he does not confess: every torturer will tell you so. And a retraction never has the same force as the original confession.

Second, in seeming (but only seeming) contradiction to this is the fact that no arrested person ever fully understands the new caution.

I have read the transcripts of many police interviews with suspects, and I have not read a single one in which the suspect has been able to explain to the police in his own words what the caution means when asked to do so. The police repeat it and ask him again, but the result is no better than the first time. Finally, the police put words in his mouth in order to pretend that he has understood.

But the menacing tone is understood well enough and the police, having started on a false footing, must be aware that all subsequent answers have been, or might have been, obtained under subliminal duress. Of course, the destruction of personal probity is one of the unacknowledged aims of the administrative state. People without probity are easier to manipulate and order about, resistless to what should not be done.

In all the cases in which I was involved, I never came across a lawyer whom I thought dishonest, except a few solicitors who refrained from paying my fee notes for far longer than they would have extended credit to their clients. There were one or two who simply did not pay at all, no matter how many reminders one sent them.

Nevertheless, they always did their best for their clients, often doing more than their duty, for remuneration which was not generous. It is true that I was involved much more with the criminal than the civil courts, where the opportunities for legalised corruption were much greater, for example by keeping a case going long after it was clear that there was no merit in it and that it could not possibly succeed. Of this practice I had little personal experience.

I had great admiration for the judges, who seemed to me to be the last bastion of cultivated English and whose decisions on points of law were delivered with an elegant clarity of argument, and with a concision as if words, like food, were not to be wasted. The acuity with which they spotted logical errors or serious omission in what counsel said or asked was impressive and, in a way, beautiful.

I loved the ceremonial of the court, the reciprocal bows of the judge and barristers. The robes and wigs that are often the object of shallow derision indicated that something solemn and out of the ordinary, majestic, was taking place. They indicated that the judge was not acting in a personal capacity, but in fulfilment of a profound duty.

A good cross-examination was also a thing of beauty, for those alive to it, though the destruction of a witness, particularly an expert witness, can be painful to watch, let alone experience.

Not long ago, for example, I watched another professor of medicine, a man eminent in his field, vivisected in the witness box in a case of a nurse who poisoned to death several patients under his care by means of insulin. The problem was that the professor, retained for the defence, had not been supplied by those instructing him with all the documentation he should have had, nor had he sought it, with the result that he had come to hasty and false conclusions which he had to retract in the light of additional information given to him in the witness box by the prosecuting counsel. The cross-examination was precise, brutal and devastating. One could easily imagine oneself being on the receiving end of it; and so long as it lasted, I found myself looking down at my shoes.

Precisely to avoid such destruction in the witness box, I learnt to be lapidary in my answers whenever possible, and never to go beyond what one could strictly defend. For advocates are past masters at casting doubt on the whole of a witness' evidence if he has made a single mistake, no matter how insignificant. *Falsus in unum, falsus in omnibus,* false in one thing, false in all, used to be a legal rule, though it is so no longer. But it is still of psychological value to an advocate trying to destroy the credibility of a hostile witness.

I once gave a talk to the annual Bar Conference on the perils of being an expert witness, amongst which is the almost inevitable temptation (in the adversarial system) to become a member of the team, either for the defence or the prosecution, for whom you are called, such that one's evidence becomes not so much a disinterested testimony to the truth of the matter, as an important, often key, element in the construction of a case. Once you have taken up a position, the temptation is to defend it tooth and nail against contrary evidence by the use of increasingly arcane and *ad hoc* arguments.

This is precisely what the professor of medicine had done. Having taken the view that there were possibilities other than poisoning to explain the patients' death, he was forced, or allowed himself, to resort to ever wilder hypotheses until they became ridiculous.

One of the events at the Bar Conference was designed to teach young barristers in training how to cross-examine. A summary of a case of diabetic coma in which there had been a catastrophic outcome (obviously based on a real case) was given to a junior barrister who was given the task of defending the hospital in which it had taken place against the charge of negligence. His witness was the late Professor Harry Keen, one of the most influential diabetologists in the country, if not the world, whose evidence-in-chief, as elicited by the junior barrister — competently, as far as I could see — was that the hospital treatment had not been at fault. The catastrophic outcome had been one of those things that occasionally happen.

The eminent QC who was to show how it was done then stood up. He hardly had to open his mouth for you to know that he was distinguished. With perfect courtesy, without raising his voice, without extravagant gesture or the employment of sarcasm, or any other rhetorical device, he managed in a very few minutes — not more than three, I think — to get Professor Keen to say exactly the opposite of what he said in his evidence-in-chief. It was both magnificent to witness, and chilling. One felt that the QC could have got any witness to say anything. If such were the fate of Professor

Keen, one of the foremost researchers into diabetes of the second half of the last century, what of far lesser witnesses? My wife and I decided we would take the QC as our advocate if we ever needed one.

It might seem, then, that trials in our system are a battle of sophists and sophisms: may the best sophist and the most plausible sophism win. And indeed it is important to have a good sophist on one's side, though a judge may redress the balance if one happens to have a bad one on one's side.

I attended a murder trial as a student, my first, in which a respectable man was charged with having stabbed his wife to death, afterwards putting his head in a gas oven (the change from fatal coal gas having already taken place). His barrister was making his final address to the jury, explaining the defendant's very hard path in life, the difficulties he had experienced as an immigrant, his battle with poverty, etc. I thought he was making very heavy weather of it when the judge leaned forward and said: 'I should have thought that the fact that his wife stabbed him first would have been sufficient explanation.'

'Yes, yes, my lord, I was just coming to that,' he said. But he obviously wasn't and he had forgotten all about it. God save us from such a defender!

No doubt incompetence springs eternal from the human mind, but I met only one truly incompetent barrister, and in his case it was because of the drink. He shook in the morning, suffered severely from gastritis, beads of sweat stood out on his forehead, and he was as swift as a rocket into the bar at every adjournment. Within half an hour of what was called 'close of play' he had consumed more than most people drank in a week. If telephoned at any time out of court, you were sure to hear pub noises in the background. My guess was that, though possessed of gallows humour, he was the lugubrious kind of drinker, the kind of drinker who stared into his glass as if it were a crystal ball.

It was no wonder that he had not mastered his brief, and that at every adjournment he would push his wig back in a gesture of exasperated perplexity (and also, I suspect, for ventilation). I couldn't help liking him though. He had that air of failure despite high intelligence and talents that I find more attractive than any smashing success.

The case on which we were engaged was not going well: if he had prosecuted Bluebeard himself he would have secured an acquittal. Just as he was about to call me into the witness box, he fell severely ill, probably as the result of his drinking, and the trial had to be abandoned. There was a re-trial, this time with an eminent QC prosecuting. Apparently the first barrister had been instructed by the prosecuting authorities in an attempt to save money — a further illustration of a law of British bureaucracy, that all its attempts to reduce expenditure increase it. On the one hand I was pleased to see the barrister go; on the other I felt sympathy for him personally, for I had grown fond of his muddle. It reassured me about my own.

Of course, heavy drinking was far from unusual among barristers. I could well understand this. After a day in court I too wanted a drink to relieve me of the tension of concentrated concentration. One barrister, already portly, rheumy-eyed and rubicund, destined to become positively Falstaffian, asked me during an adjournment whether I minded if he consulted me on a medical question.

'Of course not,' I replied, mildly flattered. 'Go ahead.'

'Is it true, doctor,' he continued, 'that whisky has been shown to cure colds and 'flu?'

'When taken in sufficient quantities,' I said.

'Thank you, doctor,' he said. 'I will follow your advice.'

Barristers were of different types, of course. There were the bludgeoners and the wielders of the rapier, the sarcastic and the secret poisoners. They could be extremely blunt and to the point, or ceremoniously polite in a way that is rarely encountered these days outside the novels of Alexander McCall Smith.

Some were so exquisitely mannered that one felt ashamed of one's own comparative coarseness. Their words were smooth and well-oiled without being unctuous. Some of them flowed from the ground up in a graceful arc, rather than merely stood. If they made you feel inferior, without of course meaning to, which would have been vulgar, it was your fault. It was because you were inferior. They were courteous even to unmitigated scoundrels and unprincipled liars. They exercised rather than exhibited their great mental power.

I remember one such who defended a man charged with murder. The facts of the case were not in dispute. The defendant was a Chinese illegal immigrant of about thirty who spoke not a word of English. He had clearly suffered from some kind of paranoid disorder, was homeless and had been wandering aimlessly in the city. There is nothing like being surrounded by crowds of people of whose language you known nothing for fuelling paranoia. Every little burst of laughter, every glance, every whisper then seems to refer to you, condescending at best and derogatory or threatening at worst.

This man's paranoia went far beyond a feeling of unease, however. He happened to meet a Chinese student in the street and fell into conversation with him, telling him that he was homeless. The student, who was married, felt sorry for him and, from a sense of national solidarity no doubt, offered him his spare room in his flat. This decent, charitable act was to lead to disaster, for the lodger soon incorporated his benefactor into his delusions and hallucinations, believing that he was plotting to kill him. He heard him, so he thought, doing so.

The 'plotting' reached a climax and, about two weeks after he had moved in, he thought that his benefactor was going to kill him that very day. He rushed out of the house and flagged down a passing police car. Of course the officers could not understand what he was trying to say in Chinese and drove on. Convinced now that there was no defence against his benefactor, he returned to the flat, armed himself with a sharp kitchen knife and when the couple emerged from their bedroom, he stabbed the husband to death in front of the wife. He then ran out of the house, but it did not take long for the police to find him.

When he was brought to the prison he was dishevelled and distracted. I could not speak to him until an interpreter was found, but it was obvious that he was responding to hallucinatory stimuli, probably voices. He did not try to communicate, even by signs, such as one might have expected of someone in his right mind. He was another prisoner in a world of his own into which what we call reality did not penetrate. It was hardly any better after the interpreter arrived: his answers were so fragmentary and nonsensical that she said she did not know how to translate them. Most of the time he simply ignored her (and me). It was an interesting sociological fact that we had to call the interpreter every time we wanted to speak to him, for though there was a considerable Chinese population in the city, there was not a single other Chinese prisoner among 1400 inmates of the prison.

A Chinese-speaking solicitor had been found for him and he sent me the outline of the case, including the fact that there had been no apparent motive for the crime such as robbery. I concluded that it was best not to make a formal diagnosis but to treat him as psychotic. To my surprise he complied meekly with the medication, perhaps from a deeply-inculcated obedience to authority.

To my surprise (and gratification) he was a changed man within two weeks. He ate and put on weight, though I cannot think the food cuisine was such as would please him. At any rate, he did not think it was poisoned. He smiled, was extremely polite and anxious to work in any way he could, for example by sweeping the floors.

We still could not communicate with him except by signs, but he soon became everybody's favourite. He was that creature of legend, the model prisoner, not, I think, from calculation but from the underlying nature of his personality or character. He told us through the interpreter that he had been smuggled into the country for £10,000 contracted as a debt that he would have to repay from his earnings. His family had sent him to England as an investment.

I informed his lawyer of his transformation, which meant

beyond reasonable doubt that his crime had been committed in a state of mental derangement. No doubt the lawyer did not need me to tell him this, but it was as well to be sure. I had known a lawyer or two miss the lunacy of their clients.

The case was a straightforward one and it took only a few months to come to trial. (The average solved murder now takes something like twenty-five times as long to come to court as it had in Victorian times. I am not absolutely convinced that there are fewer miscarriages of justice now than there were then: I have no statistics on the matter.)

The defendant must have found the English law very strange and convoluted. Before his actual trial, he appeared very briefly several times in court to be remanded back into custody. On his second appearance in court, by which time he had recovered his sanity, he removed his shirt on leaving the dock. Asked why he did this, he replied that he thought that he was going to be taken round the corner and shot. There could have been no more eloquent testimony to the nature of current Chinese justice.

When I went into the witness box at his trial, the accused inclined his head to me in recognition, a gesture I returned. He still had no English, but we got on as well as people can who have no means most of the time to communicate.

His counsel, whose every movement seemed to be on the finest ball-bearings, asked me questions with great smoothness. None of his questions was in the least awkward or antagonistic, for I was a witness to a plea of manslaughter rather than murder, a plea that the prosecution accepted at once, my evidence being uncontested.

Defence counsel read out an apology by the defendant to

the family of the deceased. No member of the family was present and I rather doubt it would have much assuaged them if any of them had been present.

The judge was now in a quandary. Normally a mad murderer would be sent to a secure hospital, where he would be treated until he recovered and then released gradually back into the rest of society, which as often as not meant living in a small rented flat where, at least in theory, he would be followed-up in an attempt to ensure that he would take his medication and did not indulge in drink or cannabis. I knew one part of the city, formerly industrial, whose main economic activity had changed from making things to looking after criminal lunatics.

It was one of the ironies of the closure of the old mental hospitals now converted into 'luxury apartments' (no apartment these days, no matter how pokey, being less than luxurious) that it had necessitated the construction of several secure hospitals, in effect psychiatric prisons, in the city, before which only one had been necessary. It was all part of the government's eternal struggle to maximise expenditure while claiming to reduce it.

The problem with this man was that he had already recovered as much as he was going to and there was nothing to treat. The judge asked me whether he would have to take his medication for ever.

'Sometimes in such cases', I replied, 'a patient does not relapse if he stops taking his medicine, but this is not an experiment that I should like to try for a very long time in this case.'

'And will he take it as directed?' asked the judge.

'He has made no difficulty while he has been in prison,' I said. (The judge was of lower rank than a High Court judge and was therefore 'Your Honour rather than 'My Lord,' and it is normally High Court judges who try murders, but some of the lower rank judges had what was known as 'his murder ticket'.)

'And will he take it once he leaves prison?' he asked.

'That depends, you honour.'

'On what?'

'On how assiduously he is followed-up.'

The judge gave me a wintry smile. He knew perfectly well what I intended to imply: that the psychiatric services were often so badly-organised or frivolous that they failed to do what it was most important for them to do. How many reports into murders committed by the chronically mad have described the almost willful incompetence of the psychiatric services, followed by administrative assurances that 'lessons have been learned' (they never have, of course, except the wrong ones, such as the development of a new form).

Like Pilate not staying for the truth, I did not stay for the sentencing, but I learned that the judge gave the man three years, which meant that he would have been out in eighteen months.

This was not much for having killed a man, perhaps, but the circumstances were exceptional. However, I could well imagine the rage and incomprehension of the victim's family on learning of this sentence. Is that the value British justice places on the life of our son? All they would have was the perpetrator's apology, which they would have dismissed as valueless and all too easily given, and perhaps some garbled account of the perpetrator's illness, which they would have dismissed as fakery after the fact, a mere attempt to evade his responsibility.

All the same, it was a humane outcome and, everything being what is and not another thing (as the great Bishop Butler said), justice is justice and not, say, crowd-pleasing, even where the crowd includes the victim's relatives.

The judge ordered that, on completion of his sentence, the man should not be deported, as normally, at least in theory, he would have been as an illegal immigrant who had committed a crime. The judge ordered this because the man would undoubtedly have been summarily shot on his return, all the more so as his victim's father was a high official of the Communist Party (and, of course, had no other child). The Chinese communists were no believers in the prohibition of double jeopardy, the idea that no one should be tried or punished twice for the same crime.

Not, of course, that Britain has, or ought to have, an entirely clear conscience on this matter. Ever since the publication of the intellectually sloppy Macpherson Report, the principle has been abrogated for the sake of political expediency.

Humbug rules the world.

16

Drunken Stress

Another killer who received a very short sentence, though in my opinion unjustly so, was a woman in her early forties who poisoned her child to death.

She was an alcoholic of more or less pathetic character who, in her very late thirties, had formed a liaison with a man, also an alcoholic, a few years older than she. Unexpectedly she became pregnant by him and had a child. They did not live together but he continued to see her and took a deep interest in his daughter. Indeed, he took his paternal responsibilities so seriously that he gave up drinking, which she did not. The couple fell out over her continued drinking, which he thought disqualified her as a mother. He therefore applied to the courts for the custody of the child. The day set for the hearing approached. It proved to be the child's death sentence.

Drunker than usual because of the 'stress' — a word that has launched a thousand excuses — of the forthcoming hearing she decided to do away with her daughter, I surmise because she knew or at any rate feared that she was likely to lose the case. She uttered to herself the most dangerous words in the language, uttered by a thousand jealous murderers, 'If I can't have her, nobody else will.'

Drunk as she was, she was sufficiently in control of herself and co-ordinated to procure her child's death by an elaborate means. She dissolved her own medicine — which was perfectly useless in her own case and should never have been prescribed in the first place — in a cough syrup for children, and fed the resultant liquid via a syringe to the child down a tube into its gullet. The child duly died, and she was charged with murder — not infanticide, because the child was much older than twelve months.

Of course, one should not let one's sympathies or antagonisms cloud or even affect one's judgment, but I found her deeply repellent in a butter-wouldn't-melt-in-her mouth kind of way, with a low-grade Mr Blair-type self-pity when accused of having done something wrong.

Although she claimed not to be able to remember events — or actions, rather — that led to her child's death, her pattern of amnesia was typical of those who don't want to remember or who think that not remembering is proof of their innocence. As in, I did x, I can't remember doing x, therefore I couldn't have done x. Sometimes prisoners on remand would say to me, 'How can I be guilty of it when I can't remember?', to which I would reply that 'If you can't remember, you're not in a good position to deny it, are you?' and advise them to change their line of defence. Their memory would then return and it was provocation or self-defence that made them do it.

The accused sobbed during the whole of the trial, or at least that part of it that I attended (and I do not think it was my presence that caused her to sob). From time to time she would moan 'Fiona! Fiona!', the name of her daughter.

It was a most irritating performance, and performance it most obviously was — obvious to me, that is. She had not been known to cry before, but in the court her grief lay too shallow for silence. Everyone's evidence was interrupted by her sobs, just to remind the jury that she was a mother who had lost a child.

The technique worked because she was found guilty of manslaughter rather than of murder, on the grounds that she suffered from a bad character, known in psychiatric parlance as a 'personality disorder'. She was sentenced to three years' imprisonment, which seemed to me little enough, derisory even, for having killed a child in this fashion.

In sentencing her to three years' imprisonment, the judge was in effect telling a lie for he knew that, as she had been in prison for seventeen months before her trial and was 'entitled' to remission of half her sentence, she would be released in a month. In other words, her sentence was eighteen months' imprisonment. The jury would not have known this and would in any case have been powerless to do anything about it.

Judges in Britain in effect connive at a fraud perpetrated on the public, assisted in the matter by the press and media who dutifully repeat that such and such an offender has been sentenced to such and such a term of imprisonment.

If the judge in this case had expressly sentenced the murderess to eighteen months, there might perhaps have been an outcry against such leniency. And indeed, since this case further purely administrative means of reducing the length of sentences have been introduced, so that the time spent, or served, bears even less relation to the judge's ostensible sentence, which is more an exercise in public relations than in penology.

It is also rather odd that having a weak or bad character should be an advantage to a wrong-doer when it comes to sentencing, at least if there is any utilitarian purpose to punishment.

The argument seems to be this: a person with a congenitally weak or bad character, such as this woman was said to have had, was less morally responsible for her act than would have been a woman of strong or good character. In other words, she was held to a lower standard of conduct than even a normal person, let alone a paragon. The worse you have been throughout your life, the more excusable your criminal act.

Now if it is alleged that there is an essential, causative relationship between a crime and the character of the person committing it, as there must be if bad character is to be regarded as an extenuating circumstance, it seems that the person of bad character is a public danger, in so far as his bad character leads him to commit crime.

On this view of the matter, a person who has led a life of crime is less likely to be reprehended and therefore reprehended less than a person who has given way to a momentary temptation of passion. As argued earlier, speculation on a person's future conduct should not be made the determinant of punishment; but it is surely perverse to punish the habitual offender less severely than the one who has one brainstorm in his life.

Perhaps we are misled or deluded, as Wittgenstein would have said, by our language. Psychiatrists and others regard character as something one has rather than as something that one is. It is a quality completely external to oneself, to which one has made no active contribution of one's own.

It is this mistaken use of language that permits a person to preserve a favourable, indeed immaculate, view of himself despite his repeated despicable behaviour. Everyone retains a jewel-like essence that is indestructible by mere conduct. No doubt in some cases a belief in Original Virtue rather than in Original Sin serves to prolong or even extend bad conduct, for nothing so crude as one's behaviour can besmirch the primordial beauty of one's soul. It follows from this that there is no need to control yourself.

Prisoners sometimes did believe in their Original Virtue, even if they did not put it quite like that. I remember one prisoner who, in a fit of drunken jealous rage, had thrown acid in the face of his then girlfriend. He claimed not to have done it because he did not remember having done it.

I asked him my usual question, 'How, then, do you know that you didn't do it?'

'Because I don't do them things.'

In other words, he knew he didn't do it because it wasn't the type of thing he did, even if he could not say exactly what he was doing at the time in question.

A little later — I delayed asking so as not to raise his suspicions as to what I was after — I enquired whether he had ever been in prison before.

'Yes,' he replied.

'What for?'

'I threw ammonia in a girl's face.'

When he said that he didn't do them things, I don't think

that he was straightforwardly lying. Nor did he see the chemical distinction between acid and ammonia as a morally relevant one. Rather, it was that the 'I' who threw the acid or ammonia was not the 'I' of his secret garden into which no behaviour could enter to affect his untouchable goodness.

He was reflecting back what I might call, using an ugly neologism, the psychiatrisation of the human condition. In my experience, though, we need Dr Johnson more than we need Dr Freud.

The case of the mother who poisoned her child was instructive to me as a stimulus to attempted thought. Those who would defend the light sentence might argue as follows. This woman's act was in particular circumstances that were most unlikely ever to arise again, for she was now past child-bearing age. Moreover her grief, if such it was, would alone prevent her from repetition of her act. As for deterrence of others, it was very unlikely that her getting away with murder would encourage anyone to do likewise, for vanishingly few people refrain from killing their children merely because of fear of punishment. Hence a longer term of imprisonment would have served no purpose and would have incurred much additional expenditure.

Let us grant for the sake of argument all the above premises (though I was not altogether sure I would choose her as a baby-sitter, in which capacity she had been in the habit of making a little money).

Does it not follow from them that the murderess should not have been punished at all, let alone for longer? After all, the premises could have been correctly advanced the very moment after she had killed her child. If punishment in her case served neither to correct nor deter, what is its justification other than a primitive thirst for vengeance?

There are philosophers, of course, who have argued precisely this, but I think that the majority of people would feel it very wrong if the woman who killed her child paid no price at all for having done so simply because she wouldn't do it again. It is a logical consequence of freeing her on these grounds that we should all be 'entitled' to commit at least one appalling crime provided that it could be shown that we should not repeat it. Once the war was over, then, there was no point in prosecuting the leading Nazis because there was never the slightest chance that they would repeat their crimes after the defeat, and most people did not need Ribbentrop to be hanged to commit no genocide. A purely utilitarian theory of punishment is untenable.

Weakness or badness of character did not always work as a mitigation in cases of murder, however. It worked in the case of the child-killer because there is a general belief that no woman would kill her own child other than in a state of great distress.

This is another circular argument, of course. She must have been distressed to kill her child, and she killed her child because of her distress. The sobs, tears and moans helped her case because we live in times that demand extravagant displays of emotion as proof that any emotion is felt at all.

Moreover, the bad character that she had displayed throughout her life was mainly of the squashed cabbage leaf rather than pit-bull variety. A hopeless character since birth — she aroused the sympathy of the jury in a way in which another murderer, a large man with a shaven head and a spider's web tattooed over his neck and one side of his face, did not.

He, too, had killed because 'If I can't have her, no one else will': a kind of signature tune.

The woman he killed came from a higher social class than he but had run away from her prosperous middle-class environment in search of proletarian authenticity. She had found it in this bull-headed man who had been a perfect gentleman to her for a few weeks before he was certain that he had ensnared her, whereupon began his jealous rages, his acts of violence, and his crude insults, followed by brief periods of contrition and promises, always soon to be broken, that he would never do it again.

He repeatedly invented a *casus belli* to justify his violence: she had spoken to another man in a pub (they were both drinkers); she looked lasciviously at a man in the street; she used too much make-up, her skirt was too short, etc. In such a situation — a very common one, as mentioned earlier — the woman devotes her mental life to finding a way not to provoke the man's violence. But there is no such way, his violence is the means by which he keeps her attached to him, and its seeming irrationality is the source of its power and effect. It has an underlying rationality, or at least purpose, which is to keep the woman in thrall to him. In nine out of ten cases its effect does not last indefinitely. The worm turns — or in this case, is killed. The jealous man does not love the woman who is the object of his jealousy. He loves himself, or rather completes himself by the domination of a woman. It is this subjection that assures him of his own significance or importance. That is why, most often, he does not stay long to mourn the passing of the 'love' when the woman leaves him. He moves on to the next woman whom he treats in precisely the same way.

The woman who leaves him should, for her own safety, make a clean break, or else his jealousy (his wounded *amour propre*) does not die down and is a spur to further violence, sometimes, as in this case, of an extreme kind. Unhappy the woman who has had a child by such a type, for the child's existence serves as a pretext for him to continue to see her. The child becomes a tool for further domination.

Alas, this man's girlfriend, having finally realised that his violence towards her would never end and that his promises to reform were not worth the breath they were uttered in, told him that she was breaking with him the following Tuesday. This was the most dangerous thing she could have done, the very thing I warned my patients with jealous lovers not to do. It is then that the thought that 'If I can't have her, no one else will', rises to his mind.

So it was in this case. She told him that he had to leave her household (which included two children by a previous jealous lover, living proof in his eyes that her affections were mutable). He appeared to agree, and on the night before the planned departure, the two of them, at his request, went for a farewell drink. In the pub she had a laugh and a joke with other drinkers in the pub. This infuriated him. They had a furious quarrel and when they arrived home he strangled her in bed.

It was by then in the dead of night; the children, away at their friends, were due home the next morning. The murderer had therefore to dispose of the body, and quickly. This was no easy matter in a small suburban house overlooked by many others. Burying her in the garden was out of the question, for it would almost certainly have drawn the attention of the neighbours. Instead, he wrapped the corpse in a blanket and, when he thought the coast was clear, deposited it in the boot of his car.

In the morning he went to fetch the children, who rode home, unbeknownst to them, with their mother's body behind them. He told the children that their mother had suddenly decided to take a holiday far away. His imagination failed him after this point and he could not think further of what to do with the body. He went to the police and confessed.

His defence was two-fold: that at the time he strangled her he had had an acute psychotic episode that diminished his responsibility for his actions and that he suffered from a congenitally bad character.

The defence called three psychiatrists. I was called by the defence late in the proceedings because the psychiatrist previously called by the prosecution changed his mind at the last moment and went over, as it were, to the defence.

I spoke to the man in the cells beneath the court before his case was called and produced an interim report unfavourable to the defence, spending the rest of the day reading the voluminous papers in the case. Having done so, my opinion did not alter, and the next day I was called in rebuttal of the defence psychiatrists' evidence.

The defence barrister, as was only natural for him to do, criticised me for the speed with which I produced my report. But I defended myself by saying that the conditions under which I had prepared it were none of my choosing and were not evidence that my conclusions were mistaken. I said that it was a combination of his jealousy, drink and the impending separation that had led the defendant to kill, none of the factors individually or in combination being sufficient in my opinion to justify a lesser charge than murder — though that, of course, was for the court to decide.

My opponents, if I may be allowed to call them such who, like me, were only helping the court, testified that the accused was suffering from a whole melange of psychiatric disorders that mitigated his crime. Sometimes in giving evidence I had the feeling that I was arguing over how many angels might dance on the head of a pin.

Defence counsel, again rightly from the point of view of defending his client, sought first to cast doubt on my probity as a witness, implying I was a hired gun. But a good advocate is both a strategist and a tactician, seeking first to put a hostile witness on the wrong foot, but also realising that he can go only so far in trying to do so. If he pushes this line too far, the jury, who usually have a prejudice in favour of an underdog as the common man (to his credit) usually does, begins to sympathise with the witness under *ad hominem* attack, and then the attempt to discredit him misfires. It can begin to look as if the defence has nothing else to say. Before long, therefore, defence counsel was obliged to move on to more substantive matters.

'You are aware, aren't you,' he asked, 'that theirs was what is called a volatile relationship?'

'Yes,' I replied, 'but she is dead and he is alive.' 'Volatile' in this context means violent, and the violence need be only on one side for a relationship to qualify as such.

Counsel moved on, down the list of questions for me that he had written down during my evidence-in-chief. He needed to establish that his client was mentally abnormal.

'It was not rational for him, was it, to have put the body in the boot of his car?'

'Well,' I replied, 'I have never been in his position myself, but it seems to me that, in the circumstances, what he did, given the alternatives, was perfectly rational.'

His cross-examination did not 'damage' me, as it is sometimes put, and he asked his last question with what seemed to me a mixture of exasperation and bathos.

'I put it to you,' he said, 'that you produced your report in haste and you do not believe what you said in it.'

This was very weak stuff.

'I agree with your first proposition, but not your second,' I said.

It was a good sign the prosecutor did not re-examine me as he had the right to do, to undo or repair any 'damage' the defence's cross-examination might have done my evidence. There was no damage to repair.

I left the court during a subsequent adjournment. As I went down the steps of the court building, the father of the murdered woman, who had gone for a cigarette, said 'Thank you' in a very heartfelt way as I passed. I smiled but said nothing: it would not have been right for me to be seen talking to him, in case I should have been accused of collusion.

Still I was gratified, for it obviously appeared to him that my evidence had destroyed that of the defence. And so it turned out, at least if the jury's verdict was anything to go by

— guilty of murder. I was pleased, for the man was horrible and had long caused misery to others, especially, but not only, women.

I thought of the father's gratitude and relief, and of how terrible it must have been for him to listen to the flimsy excuses made for his daughter's killer by psychiatrists who seemed to him indifferent to her death. How sharper than a serpent's tooth it is to have a murdered child, whose murderer is excused because he is a bad man who has behaved thus many times before.

17

Malevolent Characters

'A Poxy Little Murder Charge'

My evidence was far from over (for me) once I stepped from the witness box. I went over and over it in my mind, as I always did, finding something that I could have put better, or something that I should have said but didn't. *L'esprit d'escalier* ought really to be *l'esprit du témoin*, for I am sure that every witness feels much as I do after his evidence in court is finished. Sometimes I have wanted to rush back into court, force my way into the witness box and say, 'I forgot to mention...' Once, indeed, I telephoned the solicitor to inform him what I should have said instead of what I did say: that while it was true that many murders were committed by jealous men, most jealous men did not kill; but that when they did, their motive was usually jealousy. This I had not made as clear as I might have done. Not that they all agree that murder is serious. I once asked a prisoner on remand what he was in for, and he replied, 'Just a poxy little murder charge.'

I once had the gratitude of a man charged with manslaughter by negligence, and this pleased me greatly.

Three policemen, one of them a custody sergeant, were accused of negligent manslaughter.

A group of heroin addicts had gone out burgling and shoplifting one morning in a town several miles from their homes. In their depositions one of them said, 'We went out to work...' Indeed, it was rather like work for them because they usually left their homes at eight-thirty and returned generally after five, their 'work' done. It was part-time rather than full, for they did it only three or four times a week, scouring the houses and shops within a radius of ten miles from their homes.

That they 'worked' in this way suggests that addicts are not incapable of gainful employment, as is often supposed, and 'have to' commit crime to pay for their drugs. To burgle and steal regularly requires foresight, energy and determination, all admirable qualities in other contexts, and furthermore a commercial ability to sell what is illicitly acquired, since it is rarely cash that they steal. In a survey I conducted in the prison, I found what had often been found before, that the majority of incarcerated addicts had long histories of offending *before* they ever took heroin. No doubt their addiction gave them an additional incentive to offend, but was not at the root of their criminality.

A prisoner, a professional arsonist who burnt premises down to order, once explained to the difference between what he called a 'worker' and an 'earner.'

'Your workers', he said, 'go to the office for nine o'clock and come back at five. Your earners go out robbing and stealing.'

This gang seemed to have combined the best, or worst, of

both worlds. But one of them on this occasion was caught while shoplifting and taken down the station, where she told the custody sergeant that she was a drug addict — but not that she had taken an overdose of a stimulant drug sometimes given to psychiatric patients (which she was not) to counter the side-effects of other medication. There is a niche market for abuse of this drug.

At first the captured shoplifter was aggressive and abusive towards the police, and the custody sergeant, a man of unblemished record of service, quite properly called the police surgeon to examine her. By the time he arrived she had calmed down and he found nothing wrong with her. Having filled out the charge sheet, the custody sergeant decided to release her.

The sergeant was legally obliged to do nothing but turn her out of the police station, but she had no money on her and he ordered two of his men to take her in a police car to the border of the police area, about halfway to her home. He thought she could walk the rest, or hitch a lift. The fresh air would do her good.

His two men did as they were ordered. The border of the police area was in the countryside. That is where they dropped her off.

The custody sergeant had thought he was doing her a favour when, in reality, he was signing her death warrant. Unbeknown to them all, she was in a silent state of confusion, caused by her overdose. Instead of continuing down the road when dropped off by the two constables, she wandered off into the fields through which the road went, where she died of exposure. Her body was found several months later.

Analysis showed that she had taken a large number of pills but could not establish at what time she had taken them. The policemen were prosecuted.

I gave my evidence, by the end of which I think I may fairly say the prosecution case had collapsed. The variability of the response to the pills, and the changeability of the behaviour of addicts, from aggression to wheedling to sullenness and back again, made it difficult to assess their state of mind, and her conduct at the time of her release gave no indication that she was confused. The fact that the sergeant had called a doctor and the doctor noticed nothing untoward meant that he, the sergeant, was not merely cavalier.

When I stepped down from the witness box, the prosecution case was in ruins. The judge called an adjournment; and as I passed the custody sergeant, patently a decent man (his two men were clueless, but not malicious), came up to me and said, 'Thank you, doctor.' I had released him, almost, from months of agony and the prospect of imprisonment. Needless to say, a policeman's lot in prison is not a happy one, and if it becomes known to the other prisoners that he is a policemen, he has little choice but to seek protection in the company of the sex offenders.

His relief was obvious, as no doubt was that of his family; but I could do nothing to acknowledge his gratitude, though I would like to have done so. I nodded merely.

My sympathy for defendants was not entirely confined to the innocent. I remember a Sikh man in early middle age who had stabbed his wife to death in front of their children. It was a terrible thing to have done, but the story was a tragic and not just sordid one.

In the eyes of the law the man was guilty and nothing but guilty. The murder was his first and only offence.

He had come to England from the Punjab in his late teens and was a worker in a metallurgical factory. A marriage was arranged for him and his bride, a Sikh born in England, agreed to it.

It is important to distinguish between an arranged and a forced marriage. The former is in part an excellent system, based on a realistic appreciation of human nature; the latter is purely monstrous.

A young prisoner of Pakistani descent once complained to me of severe gastro-intestinal symptoms which did not seem very likely and for which there was no obvious explanation.

I asked, 'Is anything worrying you?' The practice of medicine is always affected by circumstances; even more so is this true of prison medicine.

'No,' he said.

'Are you sure?'

Then he told me that he was under threat from other prisoners of Pakistani descent, of whom there were increasingly many (out of proportion to their number in the population).

He had not long before been witness for the prosecution in a case of 'honour' killing, in which a man and his son were accused of having killed their daughter and sister for having refused to accept a forced marriage to a first cousin 'back home.' His evidence had been crucial in the case and was regarded by other young men of his circle as being worse than having let the side down. Rather it was treachery or treason — a threat to a whole system of which they were the beneficiaries.

For these young men, the marriages were 'arranged', but for the young women they were forced. The men approved of the system because it allowed them to live a westernised life outside the home (by which they meant common debauchery), while enjoying the convenience of a sexual partner and domestic servant in the house.

This was both convenient and gratifying, and what they thought they deserved. It was a system that needed policing so that the women did not break free of it. The system being all or nothing, my patient was a traitor and a threat and had to be punished, as indeed had the murder victim. Honour killings must go on without being undermined from the inside. I arranged for the young man to be transferred at once to another prison where he would be unknown.

Unfortunately in the case of the arranged marriage, husband and wife turned out to be incompatible, not in the sense that they quarrelled but in their fundamental ambitions in life, no doubt as a result of their different backgrounds. He was content to work hard, buy a small house and live quietly, and to achieve any social ambition he might have had through his children. He was their launch pad, as it were, providing a stable and comfortable home, encouraging them to work well at school so that they might enter the professions.

This was a noble and quietly heroic ambition. But it was not enough for his wife, who dreamed of a more vivid and exciting existence than that of housewife and mother of two children, however successful they might become in the distant future. She dreamed, rather, of luxury and, metaphorically, of baths in asses' milk.

She didn't want a little car to run around in, she wanted a

new BMW. He obtained it for her by the only way he knew, by working longer hours. Meanwhile, a handsome man of exotic origin moved in next door but one or two in the same road, and soon he and she were lovers. Her husband, whose long working hours eased their path to illicit love, found out. There was a terrible row, but he forgave her when she said the affair was over and would never restart.

But she carried on as before. She had moved on from her desire, now satisfied, for a new BMW, to a conservatory. Further hours of work were required to pay for it. But one day he came home earlier than expected and one of his children told him, with the innocence of childhood, that he had just missed the departure of the neighbour, who had been lying with his mother. This was too much for him: the floodgates burst.

He ran to the kitchen where his wife was preparing a cup of tea. He told her what the child had said. She could not deny it and said that she did not love him, that he was boring, that she needed more than he was able to provide. He grabbed a kitchen knife and stabbed her, unfortunately for his defence many times over. The children saw it all from the kitchen door. It is a mercy that childhood memories are often fragmentary, and one could only hope for amnesia in this case.

In his first interview with the police, he said that he had acted in self-defence. This was still what he claimed when I saw him. His wife had attacked him first.

Although it was not my duty to do so, I advised him against such a defence, which was untenable. The only knife found at the scene had his fingerprints on it and no one else's. Only her blood was on the knife; he, unlike her, had no injuries suggestive of self-defence. She was in any case a slight woman and he a strong man who could have subdued her easily without inflicting so many injuries on her.

Alas, the fact that he had lied in the first instance would tell against him as showing a guilty mind. But — because I felt some sympathy for him — I could not help wondering which of us would tell the unalloyed truth in such a situation.

Perhaps if he had been given the straightforward caution instead of the convoluted menacing one, he would have held his silence, he would have 'gone no comment', as the more experienced criminals put it. But now he was a liar as well as a murderer.

To 'go no comment' is by no means as easy as it might seem, incidentally. There is always the temptation to answer just one question, which is usually the beginning of the slippery slope to full, sometime overflowing, confession. The truly experienced criminal rather than the 'one-off' men, therefore refuses to answer even the most anodyne questions, such as their name. They were mute of malice rather than mute by visitation of God, as it used to be called.

The husband would have been better off with provocation rather than self-defence, though the former is only a mitigation rather than a complete exoneration, as is the former. But for provocation to have worked, he would have had to show that it was immediate and such that anybody might have reacted in the same way. Here the provocation was prolonged, the fact that he fetched the knife rather than had it ready to hand, and the repeated stabbing was against it.

Whether the law on provocation is psychologically realistic may be doubted. But law and psychology are different things, and law itself affects psychology. People will have different psychologies under different laws. When I was young the law against drunken driving was neither so tightly-defined nor as strictly-enforced as it is today and we did not take drunken driving as a serious crime, more as the kind of thing that everyone did once in a while. Now it is the only sin upon whose sinfulness practically everyone is agreed. Condemnation of drunken driving is the moral thread that keeps our society together.

The accused had appeared in the dock as the very model of the respectable man. His dark blue suit was surprisingly well-cut and he wore a red tie, properly knotted, that went with it well. He wore the suit as if accustomed to it, unlike most murderers these days who, when they don a suit in which to be tried in order to look more reputable than they are (though most don't bother), look as ill at ease in it as they would in a ballet costume.

The accused was extremely respectful towards the court. But somehow this seemed to be held against him, as if — contrary to what I believed — he were trying to give an impression that was false. He cried when he was in the witness-box, and in contrast to the woman who had killed her child, I thought his emotion genuine. He was remorseful, for he had loved his wife with an unrequited passion, and the idea that he might never see his children again distressed him greatly.

The judge, however, thought differently. Years later I learned from one of the barristers in the case that he was heard to mutter, as he left the bench for an adjournment, 'Has he stopped snivelling yet?' In other words, where I thought the emotion genuine, the court thought it bogus, and where the court thought it genuine, I thought it bogus. Inevitably, the accused was found guilty of murder.

The case struck me as tragic rather than merely sordid. The killer was not a bad man, if by bad man we mean someone who habitually does wrong. He had been overwhelmed by emotion, or rather emotions: humiliation and despair. As for his victim, she was a modern Madame Bovary. The murder was the denouement of a story that began with a mismatch, that of a couple who demanded different things of life. He had retained the first-generation immigrant's desire that his children should succeed in life, she had the second generation's desire for that success itself.

There was a case that had certain similarities soon afterwards. Every so often I was allocated a medical student who would spend two weeks with me as a kind of apprentice. A new student arrived on the ward one morning and just as I greeted him and asked his name the police also arrived on the ward accompanying a young black man whose clothes were covered in blood from a wound not on his own body.

The police wanted to know whether he was fit to be interviewed. They did not want the defence to allege that his interview had been conducted improperly.

I took him with the student into my room, the police having first ascertained that he would not be able to escape from it. He was a young Ghanaian, an illegal immigrant. The fact that he was a Ghanaian predisposed me in his favour. I had always found the Ghanaians a most agreeable of people. He smelt of dried and drying blood, however, a smell unmistakable to all those familiar with it.

It was the blood of his girlfriend — or late girlfriend. He had met her a few weeks before in London where he had found both job and accommodation, no mean feat. She had been of Jamaican descent, and they had met in a pub. One thing soon led to another and she invited him back to live with her in our city (she had been visiting London).

By now in love with her, he agreed, throwing up everything. But after a few weeks she tired of him and decided that she wanted to get back together with a former lover with whom she would compare him unfavourably and whom she would telephone in front of him, mocking his inferior sexual prowess.

Then, on the morning on which he killed her, she told him to leave her flat immediately, there and then. He pleaded with her to give him time. He had nowhere to go and no job. He had little money. He was a stranger in the city. But she was adamant and unmoved. He had to go straight away because he former lover was moving back that day. Unlike him, he would satisfy her.

Like the previous killer, he grasped a kitchen knife — one day some good soul will call for such knives to be banned — and stabbed her, though not in a frenzied attack. As soon as he had done so he called the police.

He was horrified, and astounded, by what he had done. She had played with him, treated him as a toy, and took no interest in the precariousness of his situation. He had been doing very well, in a modest way, until he met her, and then she threw him away as if he were of no more account than a used tissue. He did not mention his sense of humiliation directly, for to have done so would have been to be humiliated all over again. But he knew that he had done something terrible, and he looked blankly down at the floor.

Although he had killed but an hour before, he had a gentle manner, was soft-spoken and polite, I suspected from deep habit rather from any wish to ingratiate. In other circumstances he would have been charming to meet.

I told the police that he was fit to be questioned and they took him away. The student, a young fresh-faced scion of the middle classes, was silent and pensive. This was his first immersion in the tragic dimension of human life. I could see him mature before my very eyes.

After that interview he was no longer the same naïve young man that he had been before. There were depths to human existence that he had not previously suspected. In the modern catch phrase, this had been a true 'learning experience' for him. He had grown up in an hour.

A question of improper police questioning arose in another case. A student had been arrested outside a nightclub — one of those great caverns of youthful social conformity under the disguise of rebellion — and was found to have more of an amphetamine drug (3,4-methylendioxy-methamphetamine, MDMA, or ecstasy), than he could possibly have wanted for his own personal use. The police therefore charged him with possession with intent to supply, a dealer rather than just a consumer, which he admitted to being in his police interview immediately after his arrest.

He subsequently pleaded not guilty on the grounds that his admissions during his interview had been made while he was under the influence of the drug, admissions that he now retracted. I was sent the sound recordings of his interview by the prosecution who asked me whether there was anything in them that suggested intoxication with amphetamine or any other drug.

The interview was also sent to an expert for the defence, a doctor who, I subsequently discovered, was a prominent campaigner for the complete legalisation of other drugs. His report stated that there was nothing in the interview that excluded the possibility that the young man had been under the influence at the time.

How could there have been?

I put it the other way round: that there was nothing in the interview to suggest that he was under the influence at the time. His answers to all the questions were slow, deliberate, and to the point. There was nothing to suggest excitation or disinhibition. Rather, he was somewhat subdued, as well he might have been considering his situation.

Before the court case started, I chatted amicably with my opponent. Perhaps the defence lawyers had put their question differently to him from that of the prosecution to me. He had been asked whether there was anything to exclude intoxication whereas I had been asked whether there was anything to indicate it. Thus you get the answer you want. But here it was for the defence to prove its case.

However, this interesting question was never resolved because the student changed his plea to guilty at the last moment. His lawyer probably persuaded him that he could not win this arcane dispute, which was in any case beside the point: interview or not, the court was not going to believe that he that he had so much of the drug on his person merely for his own use.

I had the strong impression that my colleague-opponent was disappointed. An ideologue, the case for him was not really a matter of whether the hapless student was or was not a dealer, but an opportunity to confirm or establish his right to deal in what everyone should be allowed to consume.

18

Manic Mitigations

The 37.9 Per Cent

Trials sometimes turn on seemingly trivial remarks. I was not doing very well in the witness box during the trial of a young man for murder. It was a case sordid even by the high standards for such cases in general, and in particular for the city in which it took place. The accused was a homosexual prostitute who had stabbed to death an old man with whom he had gone to stay the night. I appeared for the prosecution, denying that he had any defect of mind that mitigated his crime or reduced his responsibility for it.

Defence counsel began by questioning me lengthily on an omission in my report. There was a detail I had omitted that I should have mentioned, though had I done so it would not in any way have affected my conclusion. However, the jury was not to know this, and for a time I think I must have looked incompetent at best, shifty at worst.

My mouth went dry and my voice croaky; I had to help

myself liberally to the water placed before me. My tongue almost stuck to my palate.

However, defence counsel had to move on once he had judged that he had made the most of my omission. He then presented his client as a man of such feeble intellect and will that he was but putty in others' hands.

This was absurd, in view of his life's history. At every point in his delineation I pointed to contrary evidence. His decision to become a homosexual prostitute was his own alone, for example, which — whatever its wisdom as a career choice — took some courage. But as an illustration of his client's pathetic character, he said that he would not walk home in the city on his own at night, but always insisted on someone walking with him. And, after all, he added, the city was not a war zone.

'Oh no,' I said, 'it's far worse than that.'

The court, including the judge but excluding defence counsel, collapsed in laughter. Oddly enough, the latter never regained the initiative.

I now answered his questions firmly, no longer needing the water in front of me. It was now he who needed the water. Whether it as my joke that did it I cannot say, but the jury in the end preferred my evidence to that of my three colleagues and convicted the young man of murder. (Humour must be used very sparingly in the witness box — Oscar Wilde did not appreciate this — besides which my joke was not an entirely frivolous one.)

There was another murder trial in the city soon afterwards in which I also appeared for the prosecution. It, the city, was almost comically dreadful, and I became rather fond of it.

Familiarity breeds affection as well as contempt.

The city was one of the many dispiriting British cities, formerly industrial, whose grandiloquent municipal centres had been destroyed by impoverishment and town planners, particularly the latter. They had thoughtfully provided many underground passages for the convenience of muggers and rapists, as well as those with full bladders after they had got 'blasted', 'bladdered', 'wasted', 'smashed', 'rat-arsed', 'shit-faced' (the Eskimos may have sixty-seven words for snow, we have that number for being incapably drunk). It was the kind of city in which passengers 'do runners' — running off without payment — from taxis and where the taxis are festooned with notices warning against abuse of the drivers and the fine to pay if the passenger vomits in it (the relative size of the fine being an indication of the state of the local economy). The drivers plan their routes by the proximity to them of police stations in case of trouble; and the happy young revellers 'glass' one another, that is to say push a broken glass into someone's face if he happens to look them in the eye.

A homosexual prostitute had good reason not to walk through the streets at night on his own — as, in fact, had most people.

I had to attend the trial for a week, and stayed in a peculiarly dismal hotel, a concrete block that would have gladdened the heart of Ceausescu, staffed by English and therefore slovenly, none too clean, ashamed of their uniforms which they subverted in small ways: ties undone at the collar, inappropriate shoes, badges pinned at an angle, shirt buttons undone at the midriff (usually bulging), and so forth.

Inattention to detail was complete and thorough, if that is not an oxymoron. Plate glass doors went unwiped for weeks, becoming a national park for the preservation of thumbprints; notices were posted everywhere and anywhere, creating a nightmarish visual effect, mainly about assault on staff and attempts to avoid payment. Plastic-covered sofas, mainly in that vivid orange so favoured in the 1960s and 70s, were pockmarked with cigarette burns, the smallpox of furniture; the entrance to the bar, with its loudly competing televisions, had many warnings against the use of bad language, violence, baseball caps and shorts.

On the first floor, in the so-called ballroom — a large but low-ceilinged room from which the polystyrene ceiling tiles were inclined to drop to reveal the piping and cable viscera of the hotel — was held several nights a week a church service for Nigerian immigrants or visitors. On those nights one would hear loud invocations to 'God the Fadder'. The congregation, in excess of a hundred, was composed of charming and friendly people who invited me in, but I did not want to let on that I did not share their beliefs and my acceptance might have led to misunderstanding on that score. I was reminded of a church I had encountered in Nigeria, whose name I treasured: 'The Eternal Sacred Order of Cherubim and Seraphim.' Unlike the Church of England, it used the Book of Common Prayer.

And then there was breakfast: a festival of British catering at its spectacular and hilarious worst. Although it was self-service, there was one waitress present whose role was ambiguous. She always looked as if she had arrived at work having barely escaped from an assailant through a bramble patch (which her hair much resembled). As for the food — I shall describe only the fried eggs. They had been cooked well in advance of any possible consumption. They were not so much solidified as vulcanised. They were coated in a film of whatever old lard they had been fried in and when transferred on to china from the hotplate they slipped round it like a skater on ice, evading the effort of the pursuing fork to skewer them. I had a lot of innocent pleasure from these fried eggs.

I chose the hotel because it was cheap and I was staying at the expense of the taxpayer. But I also wanted the full experience, as it were. And oddly enough, I came to love it. There were no pretension there to keep up. It gave full rein to one's inner slob.

The trial was of a woman who had killed another in a drunken and cannabis-inflamed quarrel over practically nothing. Hume said that no man ever threw his life away while it was worth keeping, but whatever the truth of that statement (I certainly do not believe it), plenty of people have thrown other people's lives away while they were worth keeping.

There was no dispute that the accused had killed. The only question was, once again, whether there was anything in her state of mind that might extenuate her crime sufficiently for a lesser verdict than murder.

At the time of the trial the law still stood that voluntary intoxication was not an extenuation. A man could not claim his own drunkenness — 'I didn't know what I was doing' — as an excuse, unless his drinking were deemed involuntary, unless he had no control over his first drink of the day. This was a largely academic distinction. In practice, it was never argued or accepted — quite rightly.

Yet again I was faced by three colleagues who had come to a different conclusion from mine. I said that had it not been for the alcohol and cannabis she would not have killed. My colleagues argued that she had an underlying character that reduced her responsibility for her actions. Once again it was argued that if your bad behaviour went on for long enough, it mitigated your next bad behaviour.

It was a kind of personality disorder that seemed to have become more frequent with the years. The *DSM5* gives a prevalence of up to 5.9 per cent of the adult population. If the prevalence of all personality disorders is calculated, then up to 37.9 per cent of us may 'have' one. According to the latest English law of murder and manslaughter, then, more than a third of the population may have a pre-existing mitigation to murder because it is now held that a mental condition has only to make a significant or non-trivial contribution to the commission of the act for the lesser charge to apply. And almost by definition, a personality disorder must make such a contribution, for:

A personality disorder is an enduring pattern of inner experience and behavior that deviates markedly from the expectations of the individual's culture, is pervasive and inflexible, has an onset in adolescence or early adulthood, is stable over time, and leads to distress or impairment.

It would not be easy (though I have done it) to argue that a person who killed had a personality disorder, but that his personality disorder made no significant contribution to his act in killing.

Was the personality disorder from which this patient was said to suffer discovered or invented? There are fashions in diagnoses, as the hems of skirts used to go up and down. They are like human rights, added by fiat but claimed always to have existed.

One of the psychiatrists called for the defence, the first of three to be called, was in private a very pleasant man, but a nightmare in the witness box. He would start off well enough, but then warm to his subject, pick up speed, and become more and more verbose until everyone in the court would begin to feel dizzy. He would start to explain and extol the way by which forensic psychiatrists came to their conclusions, a way not available to lesser breeds, issue a series of complicated statements with many subordinate clauses, including contradictions, and then list alternative and additional diagnoses. After about an hour of this, one's head spun, and when at long last he finished he left everyone feeling completely bemused. The two following psychiatrists for the defence in this case gave their diagnosis that they claimed were the cause of the defendant's act, and left the witness box immediately they had done so. By then, everyone had had enough of psychiatric explanations for the time being.

I was called in rebuttal. I said once more that, were it not for the alcohol or cannabis, she would not have killed.

Defence counsel was a bludgeoner rather than a wielder of the rapier. His method seemed to be to bully his way to the answer he wanted.

One cannot argue philosophically in court, for example the theoretical deficiencies or absurdity of the *DSM5*. In this case, however, I did not need to do so because, even by the very lax standards of its definition of personality disorder, the accused did not have one.

To do defence counsel justice, he had very little else but the diagnosis with which to defend his client. To defend hopeless cases must be almost as dispiriting as trying to teach children who do not want to learn. He was a plethoric, thin and choleric man who, oddly enough, looked younger than he was. The judge had decided to adjourn for lunch before my cross-examination began. During the break, I was handed a review article about the condition from which the accused was said by the defence experts to have been suffering. It summarised all that was known, or supposed to be known, about that condition. Everything it said was orthodox (but not therefore true).

After lunch, counsel rose to question me.

'Did you read the paper I sent you?' he asked.

'Yes,' I replied.

'Had you read it before?'

'No.'

'You hadn't?' He turned to the jury histrionically, his tone clearly indicating that I was ignorant and lazy.

'No,' I said, 'I don't claim to have read everything. But it told me nothing I did not know.'

There was no more to be gained from this line of approach, so he continued:

'It lists the factors associated with the condition, doesn't it?'

'Yes,' I replied meekly, delighted at the direction in which he was going. I knew I had him in my power.

'It says here…' and then, one by one, he read out the 'risk factors', so-called, for developing the condition, asking each time if it were not the case that she had that risk factor: and in every instance I agreed that she had.

'And yet,' he said, throwing down the paper in mock anger when he had finished, 'you say that she did not have the condition?'

I was ready for this: my heart leapt for joy, which I was careful not to show.

'With respect,' I said, 'you are like a man who sees someone smoking and concludes that he has lung cancer.'

Counsel for the prosecution sat at his desk and smirked. Defence counsel's face grew redder, almost purple. The contrast with his wig was splendid. His eyes seemed to bulge. His anger now was real.

'But she had all the risk factors, didn't she?'

'I am sorry to have to repeat myself,' I said. 'But you are getting everything exactly the wrong way round. You are making an error of logic. A man with lung cancer has it because he smokes; a man who smokes does not therefore have lung cancer.'

The smirk on the face of prosecuting counsel grew more pronounced. Defence counsel seemed unable, or perhaps unwilling, to grasp the point. He had no other point to make and sat down with an angry 'Humph!' as if it were I who had been unreasonable.

The relatives of the victim were on the outside steps of the courts as I left. One of them murmured 'Brilliant!' as I went by, and I confess I hugged myself in triumph. Once again I was struck by what must be the agony of listening to footling excuses for the murder of your close relative.

But I heard afterwards that defence counsel had collapsed and died of a heart attack a few weeks later. I was saddened to hear it, and felt a slight pang of guilt.

I was asked to see a man in his late forties who had also undoubtedly killed. The question was, as before, whether there was any mitigation on psychiatric grounds.

He was one of four unemployed habitual drunkards who formed the sort of drinking club in which the members staggered the days of their receipt of social security so that they could buy drink throughout the week. But this comradeship was only drink-deep; one of them foolishly lent another £10. This loan the latter did not repay, even after many requests, and so one day the three others decided to extract it from him by force.

The three of them went to his sordid lodgings. He let them in and they demanded the return of the £10. He did not have it. Two of them took him to his bedroom where they proceeded to beat him. But you can't squeeze pounds out of a drunk.

The man whom I was deputed to examine took no part in the beating; but when his colleagues returned from the bedroom, the beaten man cried out for help. He then went to see him. He was covered in blood, a frightful mess. 'Help me! Help me!' he moaned.

All of them were drunk as usual, as was my man. He interpreted the plea for help as a plea for euthanasia, the only help he could think of giving. He found a towel, wetted it under the tap and strangled the man as per what he thought were his wishes.

> Neither a lender nor a borrower be,
> For loan oft loses both itself and friend.

There wasn't very much that could be said in defence of the conduct of the accused, but I was surprised by how much I liked him. He had been a few months in prison and it had done wonders for him. Here was a case in which the 'Real Him', if it were more real without the alcohol, emerged. He was intelligent, personable, humorous and reasonably content.

He was not tortured by any sense of guilt, though, perhaps because the killer and the killed might so easily have changed places. His life had been a catalogue of misfortune and misdeeds; his mother had been a drunken prostitute and he had never known his father.

I would have liked to find an excuse for him, but I couldn't.

Pride goeth

Lawyers sometimes, as mentioned, don't realise their clients are mad. Quite often it would surprise them when I phoned them from the prison to tell them that their client was insane. This was not because they were unconcerned or negligent — sometimes the madness was well-hidden. I am glad to say that I never encountered lawyers who were simply indifferent to the interests of their client, though many of their clients were dissatisfied with them, frustrated at the law's delay, and (perhaps understandably) never seemed to grasp that their lawyers might have clients other than themselves.

On one occasion it was a shrewd and humane judge who stopped a trial and asked for an examination of the accused, a respectable churchgoing black woman in her late thirties, whom neither the defence nor prosecution suspected of being mad. The judge did, however, and he was right.

The woman was accused of seriously assaulting her own son, aged nearly fifteen. She hit him with an iron bar and blinded him in one eye and deafened him in one ear. She had no criminal record, and indeed was the very model of demure correctitude. The judge surmised that her uncharacteristic act did not arise out of the blue. Her cold complacency in acknowledging what she had done, without any apparent awareness of how shocking it had been, aroused his suspicion.

I met her in her lawyer's office. She was courteous and even smiling, though in a slightly unnerving way considering the situation. Mainly she was business-like and to the point, as who should say 'What's all this fuss about?'

She admitted that perhaps she had gone a little far with her chastisement of the boy, but he would not obey her or do his homework, at least to her satisfaction. She did not seem distressed that she had lost her rights as a mother. She still believed in discipline and that her son had to be set on the right path. He had to learn to obey, work hard and so forth. As to the loss of his eye: well, he had another in which he could still see, and one learns from adversity.

Although this was all very peculiar — perhaps at the extreme end of some spectrum of opinion — it was not mad in the sense the judge and I suspected. After two hours, though I was certain that if there were mad notions lurking in her brain, I had not managed to elicit them. After two hours I gave up and bade her farewell.

She stood to go. As she went towards the door, she turned and blessed me in the name of the Holy Ghost.

'So you have the power to bless me?' I asked.

And that opened the floodgates to a torrent of religious delusion. When she had beaten and blinded her son, she had done it to drive the Devil from him. A terrible tale emerged of how the Devil had taken up residence in her son and would not depart, despite her chastisement that had gone on for years. The son must have suffered terribly, mentally as well as physically, listening to her harangues, being told that he was the Devil's spawn, day after day, week after week, month after month, without ever having been able to tell anyone what he was going through, both from fear of retaliation and from loyalty. He lived in a domestic North Korea, in which madness was normality. Poor boy! Human beings can be tough and resilient if they are allowed to be, but they can also be made fragile for life. What would the boy look back on later in life? Would the state, compelled to remove him from his mother, offer him cold and minimal sanctuary, as it so often did, or would it find a compassionate soul to look after him? I know on which I should put my money. Besides, not everything can be cured or cancelled-out by compassion.

As for the mother, though she had done a terrible thing, I felt sorry for her. In her case, madness was a real intrusion, an alien force that had taken her over, as if it were she were possessed. I think she would have been a good person without it, of many good qualities.

I saw in her religious exultation — she believed that she was a prophetess and had merely been carrying out the Lord's instructions in destroying her son's eye — the shape of a lifetime of abject misery for her. I reported to the judge, who must surely have been pleased with his own acuity, and he sent her to hospital for treatment. If successful, that treatment would cure her of her delusion and she would be left a woman who had blinded her son in pursuit of mad beliefs and ruined his childhood. Insight in this case would be insight into the devastation she had caused and into her own exultant cruelty. Her return to sanity, if it were procured, would have to be handled with tact, instinctive rather than formulaic: precisely the quality that our services are designed to extinguish.

The poor woman would be cared for by a long succession of 'mental health workers', each of whom would ask her to go over what she had done, as much from prurience or even sadism as from any desire or ability to help her. Her belief that God had given her instructions directly would forever be a matter of condescension at best, derision at worst.

I remember going to see a middle-aged man in his lodgings, comparatively comfortable, who formerly had had a promising career. Unfortunately, he developed paranoid delusions and for years had believed that he was at the centre of a worldwide conspiracy. He was constantly under the surveillance of the world powers, and had been under a kind of death sentence from them from the beginning.

Over his fireplace was a photograph of a good-looking woman in her thirties and two pretty girls.

'Who are they?' I asked.

'They're my wife and daughters. I haven't seen them for fifteen years.'

His madness had driven them away. His wife had left in self-defence and for the sake of the children. Probably she had remarried. One might blame her, I suppose, for having abandoned a man so completely because of an illness not of his own making. But perhaps continued contact would only have prolonged and deepened their agony.

'It's just as well,' he said. 'They'd be in danger if they had any contact with me.'

Whoever was out to get him was out to get them too, and he loved them too well to risk such a fate for them. They were fixed in his mind at the condition and age in which they appeared in the photograph. They were thus for him in a state of permanent and unchanging happiness, and this in turn made him happy — but for the appalling conspiracy against him. Even that gave him some satisfaction. One must be of some consequence to somebody to be worth persecuting, *a fortiori* of great consequence if the world powers were doing it.

I decided against treating him. What would he have been without his delusions, even supposing he could be relieved of them, which was doubtful (the side-effects of the drugs were more certain). Without his delusions he would be a middle-aged madman who had destroyed his family by his mad ideas, and who had irreparably wasted his substance on absurdities.

Perhaps we all do it in some sort. Which of us is entirely without his illusions and even delusions, without which life is meaningless? We cannot bear too much reality.

One of the illusions (or is it delusions?) of people such as I is that of indispensability. The world, or at least the institutions in which we work, will collapse without us. To our great chagrin, they never do. They carry on. One is a pebble thrown into a pond, one makes a ripple and is gone. 'Here lies one whose name was writ in water': if that is true of Keats, what of us?

I loved being depended upon — yes, being important too — in the prison. I loved it that the officers felt they could just ask me to see a prisoner — 'he's behaving a bit odd, sir' — and I would never refuse or dismiss their concerns, which were usually justified, and even if it was the middle of the night. I cursed having to get up, but was always pleased to have done so. I loved the responsibility, the feeling that if things went wrong it was my fault, that went along with the freedom (within reason, of course) to act as I saw fit. I loved pulling rabbits out of the hat in front of officers.

One day an officer came to me and said, 'Could you see Smith on the twos, Sir. He's getting a bit mouthy' — 'on the twos' meant that he was on the second floor.

I found a man who was agitated for no apparent reason. He could not keep still, he spoke as a machine-gun spits bullets, though what he said, while mostly redundant (as is ninety per cent of human speech) made perfect sense. I noticed that he had a fine tremor, and recently he had lost a lot of weight. I thought he might have thyrotoxicosis (over-activity of the thyroid gland) and sent some blood tests away. I told the officers that he should not be charged with a disciplinary offence, though he had been repeatedly insubordinate.

My diagnosis was correct and I returned to the prisoner in triumph. He was not impressed. I told him that he needed treatment but he said, 'I'm not going to take it.' I told him the dangers of not taking it but he was adamant. 'I feel fine,' he said. I pleaded with him and offered to send him to hospital if he did not trust me. Still he refused. 'I'm not taking any bloody pills,' he replied. I went to him on successive days to check that he had not changed his mind, which was certainly clear enough for him to have the right to refuse treatment. I was defeated: 'pride goeth before destruction, and an haughty spirit before a fall'.

The prisoner was transferred to another prison so I lost sight of him. Thyrotoxicosis sometimes remits spontaneously, in which case he would have been right and remembered me as an incompetent who had tried to force unnecessary treatment on him. Wrongly, no doubt, I hoped that remission would not occur in his case, because I wanted to have been right and I thought it would do his character no good.

All careers must come to an end; and I could see that increasing administrative control would deprive my work as a prison doctor of its pleasures and it was wiser to go before embitterment set in.

The prison had improved in many ways since my arrival (I claim no part in the improvement) and some of its more absurd ceremonies had been abandoned, such as my signature affixed to the daily menu in the kitchens. What was I certifying? That the diet was healthy (it wasn't, though it was copious), that it contained no poisons, that it had been cooked in an hygienic way? No one ever told me, but I signed all the same.

But as the number of people employed in the health-care services, particularly in administration, increased so it seemed to me that they deteriorated. The more doctors there were, the harder it became for prisoners to see one.

After my service at the prison ended, I was sent a number of cases in which prisoners had been neglected to death, surrounded by comparatively giant apparatus of care. It was by now out of the question for a prisoner to be seen by a doctor at night, a change that was disastrous in several cases that came to my notice.

One late afternoon I was asked to see a prisoner who complained of a sudden severe headache. He was not the complaining type (not that frequent unjustified complaint protects against the ravages of serious disease, rather the contrary), and he was a polite young man who told me that his headache had started with what had seemed like a blow on the back of the head. This was a classic story, and on examination I found equivocal signs that he had had a sub-arachnoid haemorrhage. I sent him straight to hospital.

The junior doctor who examined him was dismissive of my diagnosis and sent him back to the prison. He prescribed an over-the-counter analgesic. I was unsatisfied, to say the least. I examined him again and sent him back to the hospital, with the demand that he should be seen by the neurosurgeon on call. He diagnosed subarachnoid haemorrhage and performed an operation that may well have saved the young man's life.

Three weeks later, the Senior Medical Officer called me into his office to show me a letter addressed to him from the young man. He thanked him for the professionalism of his staff which, he said, had saved his life; and he promised the senior medical officer that once he was released from prison, he would never return. His brush with death had caused him to rethink himself.

My mother used to say that my contact with prisoners had made me cynical. But I was not so cynical that I did not believe what the young man said in his letter, that he would not return. I do not know for certain that he never returned to prison, but I would stake money that he did not. Death sometimes gives meaning to life where it had none before. Sometimes I think that I will be let out of Hell one day every million years as a reward for having helped to redeem this young man.